A Husband, A Wife, & An Illness

Also by Dr. William July

Understanding the Tin Man
Confessions of an Ex-Bachelor
Brothers, Lust, & Love
The Hidden Lover
Relationship Reality Check
Behavior of Interest

A Husband, A Wife, & An Illness

Living Life Beyond Chronic Illness

Dr. William July

Jamey Lacy July

iUniverse, Inc.

New York Lincoln Shanghai

A Husband, A Wife, & An Illness
Living Life Beyond Chronic Illness

iUniverse books may be ordered through booksellers or by contacting:

iUniverse
2021 Pine Lake Road, Suite 100
Lincoln, NE 68512
www.iuniverse.com
1-800-Authors (1-800-288-4677)

Because of the dynamic nature of the Internet, any Web addresses or links contained in this book may have changed since publication and may no longer be valid.

The views expressed in this work are solely those of the author and do not necessarily reflect the views of the publisher, and the publisher hereby disclaims any responsibility for them.

ISBN: 978-0-595-44726-8 (pbk)
ISBN: 978-0-595-89047-7 (ebk)

Printed in the United States of America

This Book is dedicated to the amazing women in our lives who have bravely battled chronic illness:

to mom Judy and editor Judy K.—your bright loving lights and dynamic energies were taken from of this world too early by chronic illness

to grandmother Lucille and grandmother Bea—you lived long lives and lovingly gave to so many through years of ongoing pain and illness

to mom Alice—you remain a beacon of inspiration through your love and faith as you continue to seek recovery while also being a caregiver for your loved ones

Contents

"Dear friend, I pray that you may enjoy good health and that all may go well with you …"

—3 John 2

Acknowledgements

We are blessed to have wonderful friends, family, and practitioners, who have provided us with friendship, support, wisdom, and care. In no set order, we would like to graciously acknowledge: William July, Sr. and Alice July, Carolyn Caffrey, Ken and Nancy Hughes, Peggy Walton, Kim and Mike Tilton, and family, Mary Kathryn Abercia and family, Dianne and Steve Moreau, and family, Bishop Greg Rickel and Marti Rickel, Bruce and Barbara Christman, Kathy LeGros, Marlene Keeling, Yvonne Perkins and family, Frances and Patsy Scheirmann, Rev. Karen Tudor, Patsy Maner and family, Dee Sellers, Laura Lucinda McCutchin, Linda Fields, the entire congregation of the St. James Episcopal church in Austin, TX, Ken Lacy and JoAnn Lacy, Lane Atherton, Judi Knight, Matthew Knight, Dr. Joe Mills, Valerie and Danny Terrell, Dr. Greg Krenek and staff, Dr. Ron Manzanero and staff, Janet Hill, Jeff Hermann, Tony Weathersby and Bonney Harper, Meridian Grace, Dr. Stuart White and Dr. Leo Grimm, and staff, Dr. Charles Robinson, Father Paul Lockey, Dobbin Bookman, Pedro Gomez, Jami Watts ten Wolde, Nayda Flores and family, Jerry Durrett, our Northampton neighbors (awesome friends to live by), Carol Leyva, Ken Martin, Rev. Linda Shelton, Mary Robson, Rev. Jim Nutter, Rev. Kit Wallingford, Rev. Mark Crawford, Rev. Sam Craven, Rev. John Price, Rev. Kristin Sullivan, Bettye Adams, Palmer Memorial Episcopal Church (with special thanks to the Stephen and James Ministers), Rev. Irv Cutter (St. James Episcopal Church-Houston), Father Paul Keenan, Rev. Debbie Leo, Deborah Granger, Philip Yancey, Dodie Osteen, Teresa Lucher, Johnnie Allen, Dr. Guoen Wang, Dr. Patricia Salvato & staff, Dr. Carl Foster and Dr. Prima Rao, Dr. Sharon Weng, Suchetta Shah, Usha Rao, Dr. William Hadnott, Dr. Jonathan Lee, Shirin Wright, Fred King, and Minerva Cervantes & family.

PART ONE

Couples Facing Illness

Dr. William July

Introduction

The first time I sat down to write this book, I cried. For years I'd been dealing with the daily agony and challenges of witnessing my wife, Jamey, decline in health as she was struck by a devastating chronic illness in the prime of her life. I should really say *we* were struck by chronic illness in the prime of *our* lives since a marriage is a dual journey and a family is a system. When the illness crashed in around us like a massive storm, it not only changed her life but my life and my stepdaughter's as well. Our daily routines, our work, our recreation and hobbies, our family time, and our dreams had been suddenly and painfully turned upside down.

The illness that invaded my wife's body was like a violent storm that swept us far out somewhere in the ocean. When I was finally able to see clearly, the shore had disappeared and we were being tossed around by monstrous waves, holding on with nothing but hope. We were struggling to stay afloat so I rarely had the chance to reflect on it all. As I sat down to write this book and began to pull all the emotions and experiences together, it became one of those rare moments when it hit me all at once. The reality of how much devastation we had suffered was right there in front of me on paper. The words on the page unlocked thoughts, fears, and feelings that I just never stopped to reckon with.

People often ask me, "How do you handle all this?" To be honest, the answer is that I don't really have much time to sit and think about it. I don't actually avoid thinking about but I'm too busy trying to handle the losses that each wave of the illness has created to stop and consider our situation. Doing all I can to prepare us for the next tidal wave leaves no time for self-pity or emotional collapse. A soldier in the middle of a battle doesn't have time to feel sorry for himself. He has to execute the mission or he won't make it. That's exactly how I feel much of the time.

As my wife will say, this isn't a book she wanted to write. I totally agree. I didn't want to write this book at all. The old adage "necessity is the mother of invention" hit home for me. When we were still adjusting to our new reality of life with the illness, I tried to find a book that would help me as a spouse understand more about what to expect and what to do. I found a lot of books on chronic illness from the perspective of the patient, but only a few on the effects of chronic illness on couples. I was actually disappointed after reading books by other authors that did not relate to the devastating losses so many couples face when one spouse is afflicted with chronic illness. I wanted to read how someone else had dealt with the emotional pain, the financial collapse, the grief, the fears, and the social isolation. I wanted some survival strategies.

I knew I needed to write this book but I tried to avoid it because I didn't want to drag myself back through the raw emotions and stressful times that we'd experienced. But I soon realized it was a divine assignment because the words and sentences kept waking me up at night. I felt I had been drafted into doing it because the signs were all there signaling me to move forward. I am uniquely qualified on this topic because I can speak from the perspective of the husband as the caretaking spouse. I'm a nationally best-selling relationship author. I'm a psychologist. And most importantly, I have experienced this issue on a deep and personal level, gaining valuable insights that can help guide others, as they have helped me and my family. And it wasn't just for me. There are millions of other Americans out there who need insight, understanding, hope, and strategies on how to have a life beyond illness.

A chronic illness can be physical or psychological. What makes an illness chronic is its duration. The United States National Center for Health Statistics defines a chronic illness as one that persists for three months or more. A chronic illness isn't cured by an operation, medication, or a procedure. Instead it lingers for the long term, often lifelong.

A few commonly known physical chronic illnesses are: severe asthma, cancers, cardiovascular disease, diabetes, kidney disease, lupus, multiple sclerosis, rheumatoid arthritis, and thyroid conditions. Some lesser known physical chronic illnesses are: chronic fatigue syndrome, crohn's disease, fibromyalgia, graves' disease, irritable bowel syndrome, multiple chemical sensitivity, scleroderma, and sjogren's syndrome. Some chronic mental illnesses are: attention-deficit/hyperactivity disorder, bipolar disorder, personality disorders, and schizophrenia. Some lesser known illnesses fall into the category of what's termed invisible chronic illnesses. These are illnesses that may not show pronounced symptoms but are no less difficult to live with. At the very least all of these chronic conditions can radically alter the lifestyle of patient and their family. At worst some of them debilitate the person and hasten death. Consider these statistics about chronic illness:[*]

- 7 out of 10 Americans die of chronic illness.

---

[*] National Center for Chronic Disease Prevention and Health Promotion, June 20, 2007, http://www.cdc.gov/nccdphp/index.htm

- 25 million Americans are significantly impaired by chronic illness. That is more people than the total population of the entire state of Texas.

- Over 90 million people live with some form of chronic illness. That is approximately equivalent to the populations of the states of Texas, New York, and California combined.

- The number of people actually affected by the chronic illness of another person would have to include family, friends, and coworkers. That number is virtually incalculable.

With these devastating numbers it's easy to see how chronic illness is similar to a natural disaster. Except it doesn't have international media coverage and there is no urgent outcry to meet the needs of the patients and their families. Chronic illness usually strikes in the shadows inside the victim's home while the rest of the world moves on with their daily routine. It overcomes the victim and moves in with the family wreaking havoc on the entire household. Often this isn't a sudden strike, like lightening. It's usually a slow process that quietly deteriorates the quality of life for everyone involved.

That quiet erosion turned into a landslide for us. As an accomplished relationship author and media personality I made a good living writing books, presenting insightful lectures, and making media appearances on relationships. My wife was a successful business owner in personalized fitness and also wrote and spoke on wellness related topics. Life wasn't perfect but it was very good. But when the illness turned our lives upside down we would fast lose our home, investments, and almost everything we owned trying to avoid slipping under the waves. In recent years I've thought about the irony of people seeing me on television in a fine Italian suit calmly dishing out advice on relationships and current news topics, and how surprised they would be if they could see the real battles going on behind the scenes in my life.

The first section of our book is my personal journey with chronic illness as the so-called *well spouse*. As you will see there is neither ill spouse nor well spouse. There's just the reality of life with the illness for everyone involved. My intention is to provide those who are facing this battle the assurance that you're not alone and what you're going through is something millions of others can relate to. I also hope to provide the reader with inspiration and a number of practical survival strategies. Chronic illness may have changed your lives forever but it isn't the end. There *is* life beyond the illness.

Whatever Happened to that Nice Family on the Corner?

Life is made of moments. It's not always the big things you remember when you recall the good times. It's the moments, those seemingly insignificant experiences that are full of meaning. As I write this I recall one of those moments on an otherwise insignificant day. I remember sitting on a bench in my backyard rubbing one of my dogs on the head while tickling the belly of another. Then sitting back and wiping my brow from the heat and humidity of the Texas summer. I remember the sweet fragrance of our jasmine tree wafting through the air.

Your home is the center of your life. It is your place on earth, your space. To a large extent it forms who you are. Losing a home isn't only losing shelter. It's losing your lifestyle and your sense of self. Losing a home has been known to be the catalyst for all sorts of family problems because the home provides the sense of normalcy and stability.

I often wonder what people thought when they passed by our empty home as the weeds gradually took over, the little gardens in the yard became unkempt, and the pool went from sparkling blue to murky brown. Surely they saw the "For Sale" sign we had up for months. I heard one rumor that we got a divorce. Rumors always run rampant. But the neighbors who lived on our block knew we were in the fight of our lives against an invisible illness that had raided us like pirates. Our home was the first loss of many that we would experience.

I remember the last day I stood in our home. I was closing it up for good. At least for us. I'd driven back to Houston to gather up a last few items. It was so weird to see the house empty. All the memories were still there and seemed to be just as vivid as when they happened. I remembered sitting on the couch watching movies with Jamey, working out in our exercise room, and replacing the toilet tank kit in one of the upstairs bathrooms. I remembered cooking dinner together, working in our dual office, and making love late at night with the moonlight creeping in through the windows. Those memories were all so bittersweet in that last moment. While I was reminiscing a young man appeared at the gate and let himself in. I was jolted from my memories back into the present. It was the neighbor's son, whom we were paying to maintain the lawn and the pool while we tried to sell the house. We were no longer living in Houston and someone had to take care of those things.

Now our money was running low and we were down to survival expenses, food, clothing, shelter and medicine. There was not enough to continue the maintenance. I paid the young man and shook his hand. Then I told him what I knew I didn't want to say. "Chris, don't cut the lawn next week and you can stop maintaining the pool."

It was a symbolic moment. Asking him not to cut the yard or maintain the pool anymore meant our home was about to go from being one of the gems of the block to a weedy wasteland. Surely the homeowners association would be after us in a matter of weeks, threatening to cut the lawn and place a lien on the house. Worst of all, it really meant I was letting go of any hope of selling the house. It meant that if some miracle sale didn't happen soon, it would be foreclosed and we would lose our equity. I felt desperate, especially since I'd grown up in the real estate business with my family. I knew real estate inside out. We'd made a great investment in this home. It was a diamond in the rough when we bought it at a price under the market value. Jamey's creative skills and flair for design had transformed the interior and exterior into a showplace. In fact people often stopped to comment on our yard or how beautiful the house looked. Friends and neighbors were wowed when they walked in and saw the attention to detail. We'd carefully remodeled it to enhance the value without going over market value. We came home every day knowing we were already sitting on a nice profit if we ever decided to sell.

We had moved out two months earlier because we knew if we didn't get a sale on the house soon we'd lose it in foreclosure. We could no longer pay the mortgage and the cost of renting another home while paying medical bills. It was time to sell the house and unlock our equity so we could start over.

When chronic illness hit our lives it hit us hard and fast. Everything that could go wrong did go wrong. The first signs of something going wrong were subtle. But when Jamey and I reflected on these things we almost thought there was a metaphysical pattern to it all. We jokingly called them the four plagues.

The Four Plagues

I now look back at the beginning of our problems as heralded by what I call the four plagues. It was one of the weirdest sequences of events I've ever experienced in my life and I hope to never have it happen again.

First there was a hailstorm with hail the size of golf balls that pelted down covering the patio, yard, walkways and damaging our roof. We didn't think much of that. The roof was getting old and was about to need replacement anyway. Besides, it was covered by our homeowner's insurance so we didn't worry about it.

About a week later the pump on our pool broke. Within a few days I began to see algae creeping along the walls. We didn't have the money to fix it for a month and before we knew it, algae was growing out of control everywhere. That's when the frogs decided our pool would make a great summer resort. First a few frogs took up residence. Soon there were so many frogs the sound of them at night became unbearable. Our daughter's bedroom looked over the pool and she could no longer sleep because of the incessantly loud chorus coming from the frogs

Finally, we got the pump repaired and it was time to reclaim our pool. But before I superchlorinated the water, my wife and I went out with a fishing net and caught the frogs. It took us more than an hour to get every one of them out of the pool and the surrounding areas. We had enough frogs to fill two large garbage bags. I drove down the street to little park in our neighborhood and walked down to the banks of the pond and poured the frogs out. Panicked and excited, they leaped off in every direction. Some jumped into the pond. I got a chuckle from it. That night our backyard was nice and quiet. Problem solved.

But then the next plague started and it was the worst of all. Our neighborhood was an oasis set in the midst of a large wooded area so it wasn't unusual to see all manner of birds, skunks, squirrels, rabbits, and deer roaming around right into backyards and onto streets. But that also included rats. Rats were not uncommon because they'd come out of the woods and feed on whatever they could find. They apparently found the composting spot in the back corner of our yard. I also suspect they may have helped themselves to the three food bowls set out for our dogs. Their next move was into our garage where they built nests and made themselves right at home without being detected. From the garage they found a route across the breezeway into the walls of our home. Then they ingeniously made their way to the attic and set up a colony. I didn't know the house was infested until one day when I was cutting the yard and I saw a dead rat on our roof. Following a hunch, I went into the attic. I was astonished. The attic was filled with rat droppings and gnawed paper, and I found a couple of dead rats. I searched for more evidence in the garage and found rat droppings. As I moved a few boxes, a huge rat jumped out and ran straight up the wall. It scampered across the beams of the ceiling and disappeared right into the space over the breezeway. At that moment I knew it was headed for the attic and we had a real problem. I also realized the rats had been living right there in the garage and had a well-established route through our walls and into the attic. It was creepy and I felt dirty and violated by the vermin. We paid a rodent control specialist to come out and rodent proof our home. He found all sorts of hidden places where rats could enter the house. He set traps, built screens, and covered holes, but the problem seemed to persist.

To this day I believe our story really begins with rats. In fact, I still think the rat infestation we experienced has something to do with how my wife got so sick. Jamey was already managing an atypical lupus condition so any rodents with germs or fleas were a prescription for disaster. Her immune system was vulnerable. Rats are known to be vectors for all sorts of diseases. Rats caused the bubonic plague in Europe that wiped out a third of the population. In my gut I feel they were the vector for whatever eventually affected Jamey. My hypothesis is that since the rats had infested the garage where our dogs slept, they'd infected the dogs, perhaps through fleas or by biting them. Also, they were spreading germs, mites, and fleas inside the walls of our home which would come out and affect us. Although, I can't prove this, I've done a lot of research that makes me very suspicious about it.

Before we knew it Jamey was itching insatiably and that was the beginning of the fourth plague. I was experiencing the itching too but I'd describe my bouts of itching as a minor irritation. It was Jamey who was getting eaten up by something. We had a flea company come out and do a special process, and it worked for a while. But then the itching started again. We had the carpet cleaned. That worked temporarily. We vacuumed every inch of that 3,300 square foot house every day. We went up walls, behind pictures, under furniture. Still, the itching was getting worse.

Things started getting out of control fast. Jamey was getting worse. We became a single income household and we didn't have health insurance. Now our money was going out faster than it was coming in. Within a few months we put the house up for sale and we started selling off furniture to pay the bills. We figured it was just a stopgap measure until the house sold. Realtors paraded in and out but we found out people were opting for the newly constructed homes down the street which were just coming on the market. We never got a sale so the home was foreclosed and our equity went down the drain. We were counting on that money to make a new start.

By that time we were living in a Central Texas town where one of Jamey's family members lived. This relative had recently gone through a divorce and was fighting breast cancer and other family members for various reasons were unable to go and stay with her through the ordeal. Looking for a place to relocate and start over we chose to move there and help Jamey's loved one while we reorganized our lives. We also thought the dry air in Central Texas might help

Jamey's bizarre skin condition. We rented a home in a neighborhood close to Jamey's family member. The plan was to stay in the town until my wife's relative had completed her chemo treatments, and I finished my master's degree, and then move to Austin.

I still had hopes of selling another book and pulling us out of the nosedive. One book sale could have changed everything and since we lost our equity we really needed it. But the most infamous attack in American history put a stop to that. When 9 11 happened I was substitute teaching at a high school in the small town we were living in. I watched the towers burn on television and had no idea that my next book deal was burning too. After 911 the last subject on the minds of American publishers was relationship books. The mood of the nation was somber and I couldn't get anything sold.

Suddenly, we seemed to have lost everything. I think we spent that entire year in a state of shock. We'd lost our home, our cars, much of our furniture, and we'd even had to part with our beloved dogs. It was one of the worst years of my life. I'd never felt as confused, angry, and hopeless as I did then. As the one year anniversary of our stay in the small central Texas town approached, I finished my master's degree and we moved to Austin where I started two new jobs, both at nonprofit agencies. I also began working on my doctorate that year. With all that and Jamey's health rebounding, things were looking up.

I wished the story went from there to another stage of happiness but it didn't. Our short renaissance in Austin was abruptly halted by a major downturn in Jamey's health. This time the road would lead us back home to Houston, where my parents had a home large enough to take us in. It was time for family to pull together. I needed someone to help me take care of Jamey, and my aging parents needed me there to help them. Sometimes God works in mysterious ways. My plan A had failed. Plan B went up in flames. Now I was on plan C and it was probably the best of all. Back home in Houston I was able to find a great job as a university professor while also being able to help my parents and receive help caring for my wife. Finally, things slowly started to stabilize.

Action Plan

1. Realize what is happening to you

Early in the process of things starting to slip away, I realized "Oh my God! If this keeps up we could lose everything." Quickly, I started taking steps for a plan B, and even plan C. Good thing I went as far as C because that's where we ended up after plan B played out quickly.

2. When you're in battle there's no time to be a philosopher

The place you're in at first is a place of reaction. There is no time to sit back and reflect. It's time for action. You have to take action and it has to be decisive. This is not a time at which you even have the luxury to stop and feel sorry for yourself.

3. Remembering the good times is good for you

Keep remembering the good times you had. After a while, memories seem to be all you have. Remember them because they will give you hope and inspire you. They will let you know life can make sense. I still remember the jasmine tree we planted in our backyard. That's one of the things that I think of when I remember the way things were.

Questions to Consider

1. How do you maintain hope when you lose so many things that mean so much to you?
2. What are your plans for living a life beyond the illness?
3. How do you maintain a sense of balance when everything in your life seems to be falling apart?

Journal Idea

What are the good moments that you remember before the illness?

Ready or Not, Your Life Has Changed Forever

Remember how as a kid you played the game of hide-and-seek? Fair warning was the key to a good game. The seeker had to close their eyes, turn around, and count to ten. Then before starting they had to shout, "Ready or not, here I come." It gave you that last moment to prepare. You'd hunker down in your hiding place, wiggle back into a corner, or just take off running at full speed. Whatever it took to get away and not get caught.

A critical part of your preparation and strategy was the fact that you knew you had time to get ready and you always received that last warning to prepare. Unfortunately we don't get that same warning as adults. There are no rules for the snares that can trap us in the game of life. There is no count-down clock, no out-of-bounds or final warning.

Chronic illness doesn't give a warning before it seizes the life of a couple. For some it slowly creeps up like a shadow and swallows them. For others the onset is sudden and immediately devastating. Either way you don't see it coming.

The onset of disease, chronic illness, disability, and mental illness are all events that radically change the life of a couple. In our case, it's a severe chronic illness with no known cure. Illness changes a couple's life forever in four ways: (1) it derails major plans, (2) it radically alters your daily routine, (3) it puts a tremendous strain on finances, and (4) it is a source of emotional strain.

I can think of many ways chronic illness has derailed major plans in our lives. But probably the most poignant and painful loss is our plan for having a family. Jamey has a daughter but I have no children of my own. When we married, we planned to have a family and experience the joys and pains of parenthood together. But first we wanted to get settled, build our nest, and work on our careers. I'd just published my first book, which had taken off like a rocket, propelling me to some major best-seller lists. It had also created a steady stream of media opportunities and offers to speak all over the country and abroad. Jamey was working on a book and also doing speaking engagements that focused on health and wellness topics. At some events we were even able to be on the same program. Our passion for our work and the opportunity it gave us to reach out to others often prompted journalists who were interviewing one of us to ask if they could include the other in the story. For example, when a major newspaper did a feature on my work as an author, they also talked with Jamey. As a result the feature developed into a story about us as a couple. Likewise, when a New York-based filmmaker came to Houston to interview Jamey for a documentary, she brought her crew back for several more takes and asked if I would sit in with my wife for the final interview. At one point, the cinematographer poked her head out from around the camera and said, "Wow. You guys are so interesting and great together on camera!"

This was just a reflection of our love for each other and our enthusiasm for life. We were truly blessed to have each other. With our careers in full swing and time on our side, we laid out our plan to adopt a child and hopefully to have a biological child after that.

We had a beautiful home with a backyard like a private park complete with a large swimming pool. We loved working in the yard and gardening. Thanks to Jamey's green thumb we had flowers blooming year round and the calming scent of jasmine, roses, or gardenias was always present in our home.

We had bought this home with the idea of having space for all of our children—the one we already had and the two to come. We had enough bedrooms for each to have their own room with even an extra bedroom for visiting family and friends. I always felt Jamey would be a great mother for our future kids. She was already a great mom to her daughter. She's exactly what I wanted in a mother for my children: kind, maternal, smart, funny, and savvy in business. I also loved her genes—she had a beautiful face, and in addition to being an athlete she could sing, act, dance, and was quite an artist.

Our neighborhood was a perfect place to raise a family, and our neighbors soon became friends. We had some great times having our neighbors, friends, and family over for holiday gatherings and summer cookouts. Some of our most memorable times were the summer evenings when we enjoyed walking our three "furry kids" down the beautiful esplanade under the tall pine trees that ran through the neighborhood and past the golf course. Another great memory is being pleasantly surprised at how high school kids would go around the neighborhood singing Christmas carols every year. And on the Fourth of July there was a neighborhood parade for the little kids. They decorated their bikes and made little floats that went down the main boulevard. The last year we were there I remember standing on our porch watching the parade go by and thinking, "Soon I'll be out there with our kids." I also had dreams of being a Little League coach for our son's football team or our daughter's soccer team.

We lived in one of the best school districts in the state with award winning elementary, middle, and high schools about 5 minutes down the street. We had also begun looking into adoption agencies because we both wanted to offer our love and home to a child in need. We felt especially blessed that we were doing well enough to give to our favorite churches and charitable causes. I guess you could say we were living the American Dream.

We had no warning or way to know that our dream was about to turn into a terrible nightmare. Jamey had been through a serious bout with Connective Tissue Disease (CTD), fibromyalgia, and an atypical form of lupus years earlier but thanks to her knowledge of nutrition, exercise, and holistic treatments, including deep tissue therapy and acupuncture, these conditions were well managed. She was working part-time writing and presenting lectures and workshops while creating a comfortable home for our family. Suddenly, everything changed. One week-end while I was in Los Angeles doing a television show, Jamey enlisted our housekeeper's son to help her bathe our three "furry kids." One of our dogs, Bearun, had been ill with a nasty chronic ear infection and skin condition so my wife took special care to bathe him herself. That night, she began to experience a bizarre series of symptoms. Over the coming months she endured fevers, night sweats, and a red burning inflammation of her scalp and skin, along with rashes and lesions that caused incessant burning and itching and created allergic reactions similar to an asthma attack. As we sought doctor after doctor for a diagnosis and treatment, we inevitably ran into dead ends and frustration. I watched helplessly as my wife's health, energy, and vitality slipped steadily away.

As time passed, more strange symptoms accrued and Jamey's health continued to worsen. But this bizarre mystery illness that we now faced was not finished wreaking havoc on our lives. Because we were both self-employed (and because Jamey had previously been diagnosed with CTD due to the fibromyalgia), we had been unable to get any health insurance for her. So now, the expense for every doctor and every test and medication was coming directly out of our pockets. With Jamey unable to work and part of my time now devoted to helping care for her, our financial status took a nosedive. In addition to the physical loss that the illness exacted from my wife, our grief and frustration were compounded as we eventually lost our beautiful home, then forced to sell our cars, favorite antique pieces, and other valuable possessions. I think the final blow was that we could not keep our beloved pets due to my wife's condition and weakening immune system. It was a sad, sad day for us when we had to say good-bye to our dogs, for they had been a part of our family. But we had little time to grieve as we faced the challenge of battling for my wife's life.

This Is Not a Reality Television Show

The popularity of reality television shows is due to the way they allow people to vicariously experience the world of someone else without actually having to face the consequences. This allows people to experience their fantasies as well as their deepest fears without leaving the comfort and safety of their sofa.

We'd make a good reality show. You have the author and speaker, doubling as a professor, balanced against the husband who cares for a chronically ill wife. You also have the wife, a wellness expert who was a competitive athlete, facing pain combined with the mental and physical fatigue that comes with a major chronic illness. But chronic illness is not a reality television show. We can't just change the channel. It's all too real to those who experience it, and to their families. It doesn't start and then stop. It doesn't end when the director says "Cut!" There's no special editing or magic pill to make it stop. Chronic illness is something individuals and their families have to come to grips with because they may be living with it the rest of their lives. It's like being sucked up by a giant tornado, then being hurled back out twisted and broken, and landing in a strange place. It involves major losses on every level. Your spouse loses his or her physical health, energy, and even their appearance. As I've stated, part of the irony of my wife's condition is that she is a wellness expert, a former athlete and fitness model. But she has become swollen and disfigured from the effects of the illness and the medication. I'll discuss that in more detail in a later chapter.

The spouse with the illness feels they have lost many things, and perhaps their very identity. Here are some thoughts and feelings of the spouse with the illness:

- Low self-esteem, resulting from the feeling that they are worthless or a weight on their spouse or family. Some even think, "They'd be better off without me."

- Guilt, resulting from their inability to contribute, or their having to depend on others.

- Isolation and loneliness. The chronically ill are inevitably left alone for long periods of time while everyone else goes to work or to other activities. Feelings of frustration and desperation can easily grow at these times.

- Excessive worry about things such as finances. This worry is compounded by the feelings of guilt the ill spouse has about not being able to contribute financially, and being the source of bills for doctor's visits, medication, therapies, etc.

- Frustration from feeling life is passing them by as they lie in bed too ill to get up and participate in daily activities. The feeling of being trapped inside a nonworking body is common among those suffering from a major illness.

- Doubt, on the spiritual level, about the meaning of their existence, the value of their life, and whether God has forsaken them. It is not unusual for the chronically ill to have major philosophical crises.

But the so-called well spouse is not a mere spectator. In psychology there is a phenomenon called the bystander effect. It is essentially the behavior of people watching something, such as a person needing help in an emergency, and not taking action because they feel someone else will. Therefore, no one takes responsibility and nothing gets done. In chronic illness the spouse cannot be a bystander. As the spouse, you're experiencing your husband's or wife's loss as well as your own form of loss from the illness because it affects you and your relationship profoundly. Here are some thoughts and feelings of the so-called well spouse:

- Emotional and spiritual pain of watching someone you love suffer when you can't help them.

- Mental and physical fatigue because you have to earn more money. You've likely had to work more hours or perhaps you've even had to take two or three extra jobs. Basically you have to work triple duty. You have to generate your regular income, additional money to compensate for your spouse not working, and even more money to feed the bottomless pit that the illness creates.

- Loss of vitality, which often affects the mate of a chronically ill person. They may gain weight or find themselves so tired from the cycle they live in that they only go to work, come home to the role of caretaker, then go to bed exhausted. In this cycle they inevitably don't eat right or get enough rest, so their immune system can become compromised from the stress.

- The psychological toll for the well spouse includes worry, guilt, and also feeling life is passing them by. For example, the plans you had for your life and career that have been interrupted.

- Also, some spouses have the challenge of parenting the kids while taking care of a spouse, working, and managing the household.

Action Plan

Chronic illness has profoundly changed your life and your relationship forever. It can ruin lives and relationships can be ruined when people don't take the time to learn how to manage the situation. This doesn't mean things will never be happy again.

Life can, and will, be good again because you are investing time and energy into making a way for this to happen. But you, your spouse, and your family are going to have to acknowledge and accept the circumstances. You must strategically plan to manage the challenges presented by this new life. The following list will help you do that. And for those who are already living with chronic illness, injury, or disease, this list can help you fine-tune your management of the situation.

1. Create a New Normal

What you knew as normal is gone. It probably didn't just suddenly disappear either. For most of us it just slipped away. It begins with slight changes in lifestyle, such as not being able to go out to a restaurant or taking into consideration the extra details it takes to travel anywhere. I can't really pinpoint when our normal life slipped away because it happened so subtly. Normal doesn't storm out of the room and slam the door. It slips away piece by piece. Day by day, little routines change. Set routines disappear because of new demands. You may not even recognize that these are no longer part of your life.

Much of our initial frustration was because we were in limbo between what we considered our "normal" life and the world of chronic illness. We thought surely this experience would end soon and things would be back to normal. Well, things never did get back to normal. Instead they became more and more bizarre. It took us almost about two years into the illness to accept that our old normal was gone. Finally, we realized that the life we were living *was* our way of life. A long grieving process followed that. But that was the biggest turning point for us as a couple and as individuals. We made peace with what we were going through. The resistance stopped and the flow of life and living returned. Note, I'm not saying we stopped looking for a cure or that we gave up hope. Don't ever lose hope or stop looking for healing or ways to lessen the severity of the condition. What I'm referring to is that there has to be an acceptance of the fact that things are going to be very different. Make peace with that and you will have set the foundation for a life beyond illness.

This redefining of "normal" is very important. It's a fight for your life because the chronic illness lifestyle will creep in and take over if you don't actively work to have meaning and purpose in your life other than just going to doctor's appointments, taking medications, discussing the illness, reading about the illness, and having anxiety about the illness. Fight for your life AND your well-being!

2. Don't worry while you work (for the well spouse)

In both my professions the theme is giving of myself. As a university professor my job is to deliver information to my students. In that role I also give of myself as teacher and mentor. I realize that what I do can greatly affect a student's self-esteem or even whether they continue in school. Therefore, this role is not something I take lightly. I have to maintain a high degree of concentration from the minute I step on campus to the minute I leave. So at some point I must psychologically shake off the role I play as the spouse of a chronically ill wife and be able to absorb my present role and radiate in it. For me the prep time is on the drive to the campus. During the 30-minute drive I have plenty of time to mentally shift gears. I'll listen to sports radio, jam to some jazz, or listen to a speaker who can enlighten me on some subject. I look forward to this drive time and it's a ritual for me as I transition into another role.

As an author and professional speaker my words and my energy are my product. If I write morose and depressing books, people won't buy them because I am not helping them get beyond their own rough spot. As a speaker, I don't get flown in and paid well to stand on a stage and remind people of how bad things are. My job is to inform and to inspire. So if I'm to do that, I have to grab the bull by the horns. I have to face this illness in my wife that has taken hold of our lives and figure out how I can make it a positive experience not only for Jamey and me but also for as many people as possible. By doing that I am in combat with this monster and I am defeating it. The more I am able to transform this experience into something positive for myself and others, the less powerful it becomes over us all.

People sometimes ask me how I seem to be so positive in spite of what I manage on a day-to-day basis. It isn't so much that I'm insatiably optimistic, because I'm not. Like anyone else I have times when I'm down in the dumps. Nor do I walk around with rose-colored glasses. I am coldly realistic and anyone who knows me knows that. I just don't dwell on the negatives. I suppose the difference is that I see chewing on negative thoughts and ideas as just a way to create more negative thoughts and ideas. So if and when I go there, to the negative thinking place, I go there only temporarily, to vent. After that, I have to get back into the game of life. If I wallow in negative thoughts, they grow and become insurmountable walls in a dark canyon with no visible path out to the top. Negative seeds grow negative weeds!

3. Coordinate valued activities into your routine

Living with chronic illness requires a routine. You, your spouse, and anyone else in your household or close circle of family and friends, are all affected by it. Another thing you will have to do after your normal slips away is to learn how to include your usual activities into the cycle of chronic illness. In other words, you'll have to fit your life around the illness in order to have a life beyond it. This is very important because if you don't, you may lose both your identity and your sense of purpose. From there you can lose your essence and vitality and become only the shell of a person.

If you're the spouse with the illness, find ways to do something constructive each and every day. Hang on to any piece of the normal world that you can. Due to your condition you may or may not be able to do certain physical activities. But find something to do that connects you with the rest of the world. Through several support groups, my wife has made herself available to speak by phone with others who are experiencing chronic illness, and is especially able to offer insights to those who have some of the conditions she has suffered from. Most of all, she is available just to listen and to pray with the person in need. On her better days, we go to the park and walk or, if I'm teaching or otherwise busy, she goes out with a friend for a walk; afterward they stop and visit over their favorite hot tea. In the past year, she has begun to write again using one of her God-given gifts. This stirs up endorphins and positively impacts her healing. On the more difficult days, she may be restricted to bed but she usually phones a friend or sends out e-mails. She also has inspirational and spiritual audio CDs that she listens to when her symptoms are most prominent.

Likewise if you're the well spouse and you like working out at the gym, keep doing it. If you watch old movies late at night, find a way to keep doing it. If you like to play softball, stay on the team. This is critical. You can make the schedule work if you put some effort into figuring it out.

4. Don't Live in A Sick World

Remaining in the mainstream is a psychological and spiritual high ground that you must protect. With your spouse surrounded by illness, you are the one who has to defend the ground to keep your lives from becoming a mere function of dealing with the illness. The world of illness is not where you want your mind to be. If you slip completely into that world of illness it would be like a pilot losing the instruments at night or in a storm. Remember, you may have to live with the illness, disease, or injury, but you don't have to have a sick life.

Many people with disease, physical challenges, mental illness, and chronic illness live rich, full lives. It's not easy and it requires an immense amount of preparation, but they do it. They actively fight to stay in the mainstream. I once had the pleasure of speaking at the same event as Bill Irwin, a blind man who astonished the world by walking the Appalachian Trail. Jamey and I were fortunate to talk with him and his wife for about half an hour after the event. He had a calm and solid peace about him as well as a lot of wit and humor. Then there's Jason McElwain, the autistic 17-year-old boy who scored 20 points in a high school basketball game. The list could go on.

To avoid living in a sick world, transform your mind. Keep visualizing a better life! Your visualizations can be simple or elaborate, it's up to you. For example you could meditate on the idea of your spouse waking up pain free, or having an entire day without pain or symptoms. Others may want to visualize their spouse physically looking healthy. Research has shown that positive memories have a tremendous power to give us hope and a psychological boost. Harness the power of good memories. I often think back to the beautiful home we had, with its manicured lawn and park-like backyard, and to swimming in our pool as we gazed up at the beautiful sky and circle of tall pines above us while our dogs playfully ran around the pool and tussled with each other. The power in that vision is that it reminds me of where we can be again. It reassures me that things don't have to stay this way. The lifestyle of the illness isn't our destiny, only our present state, and we choose to see it as a step toward something better.

5. Set A Personal Goal

For me the goal was to continue graduate school despite the situation. I didn't want to let the illness rob us both of our vitality so I stayed in school. I had just begun my master's degree when Jamey started getting ill. Playing the roles of caretaker, sole income earner, and grad student was very hard on me. But with perseverance I completed both my master's degree and Ph.D. in five years.

That goal helped me keep one foot rooted in a non-sick reality, which preserved my sanity. It wasn't easy. But in an odd way the additional stress was offset by the escape I had by going to school. The illness didn't make sense. It wasn't logical. It didn't have a starting and ending point. It was an abstract monster. The master's and doctoral programs, in contrast, were finite. Though rigorous, they had definite starting and ending points. They made sense and I moved along at a controlled pace that gave my life some order and meaning during a time I could've easily become obsessed with a negative situation, which would not have been healthy for me.

Questions to Consider

1. How have your goals for your life changed since the onset of the illness?

2. Despite the illness, what are some really good things in your life right now? Keep thinking of items until you can write down at least seven. Take this list and tape it on the wall in front of you where you pay your bills, or at work.

3. What are some ways you can fit the duties of your role as the caretaker into your regular life and vice versa?

4. What is a major goal you have that you can still achieve despite the pressures of being a caretaker? Make a step-by-step plan to achieve that goal.

Journal Idea

When did you realize that your idea of a normal life had changed to include the presence of the illness?

No Health Insurance?

Want to hear a joke that isn't funny?

A patient is sitting in the exam room talking to her doctor. The patient says, "So, doctor, what's wrong with my body?"

The doctor is looking perplexed and rubbing his chin. "Well, you have a lot of symptoms but none of it fits into a category so I don't know what to tell you. I can't diagnose you with anything that I know of."

The patient leaves the doctor's office and goes to the insurance company. The patient says, "I need a health insurance policy."

The insurance company asks the patient for her health history. After using four additional sheets to list everything, the patient gives the forms to the health insurance company. The company representative's mouth drops open and he says, "We can't insure you due to your health history."

The patient says, "But the doctor didn't diagnose me with anything."

The insurance company replies, "Yea, sure, but you're obviously ill. Well, okay. We'll do you a favor. We'll exclude coverage for every possible illness that could occur from that four-page list of symptoms and insure you at the maximum rate allowable. Will that be cash or check?"

I told you it wasn't funny. And it's confusing too.

There's nothing funny about being a middle-class American with no health insurance. We've been there. If you're poor you can get government assistance. If you're rich you can pay for it out of pocket. But if you're middle class and you have no health insurance, you're in for a big surprise. Worse, if you're middle class and you have your own business you can hardly get insurance even if you can afford it.

I'll never forget having to take my wife to a county hospital because we didn't have insurance. As writers and speakers, we had our own successful business but couldn't get coverage because of her pre-existing conditions. We sat on hard plastic seats under bright fluorescent lights while being blasted by a loud television mounted on the wall that spewed out mindless garbage. This ordeal went on for 12 1/2 hours as we slowly moved from one waiting room to the next. A nun who was sitting next to us had been there 14 hours. Her complaint was pain she was experiencing from a brain tumor. But that wasn't enough to get her in to see a doctor immediately. She was waiting along with the rest of us. It was triage care, if you weren't literally bleeding to death, you just had to wait.

Finally, we'd had enough. I couldn't stand seeing Jamey in so much pain, just sitting there suffering. She was trying to maintain her composure but I could see the pain and sadness in her eyes. She seemed on the verge of collapsing and we both thought it would've actually been better for her to do that at home in bed than to sit another hour in the waiting room. If it came to that, at least that way we could call an ambulance and she'd move to the front of the line.

We got back into our minivan and made the 45-minute drive back home to the suburbs. When we got there it was like arriving in Shangri-la. The sun was coming up on the lush, pristine lawns, many of which had sprinklers gently raining on the grass. This was a striking contrast to the dingy waiting room and the bleary lights we'd been in all night. When we turned the corner and saw our home it was a relief that I can't even find words for. But little did we know the financial price we were about to pay as we unwittingly began our descent into the world of chronic illness without insurance. We would no longer be able to afford that home and it would soon become just a memory, along with our entire way of life.

Though not having health insurance caused a major financial crisis for us, I'm not intending to imply that health insurance assures a cure. For the chronically ill, health insurance doesn't provide a cure because what they have either isn't on the charts or is often misunderstood, ignored, or even misdiagnosed. Yet health insurance is still a valuable tool for prescriptions, visits to doctors, procedures, surgeries, hospitalization, emergency room trips, and the like. Even though it may not lead you down the road to a cure, it can certainly make health care accessible and much more affordable.

Action Plan

1. Get health insurance through a group

Your best option is to find a job that provides group insurance. Most full-time jobs, and some part-time jobs, provide health insurance. The value to you is that you can be covered as a member of a group, which reduces your rates and, more importantly, increases the chance of your spouse's illness being covered without a lot of exceptions.

You may belong to a professional association or some other type of group that offers group health insurance coverage. For example, I read on the website of a professional organization of which I was a member, that a group insurance plan was available. So make sure you investigate this option.

2. Find out if your state has a health insurance pool

Many states provide health insurance pools for which the state subsidizes part of the premium so individuals with severe illnesses are assured coverage at an affordable rate. This allows people who would ordinarily be turned down due to their health history to obtain insurance through major insurance companies. If you can pay the premium, this is an option.

3. Pre-register for public services

If you don't have insurance, get registered for the public clinics. Some public clinics provide good health care but you have to fill out the paperwork. It can be a lengthy and challenging process. Get this done in advance so you can have access to the local public clinics operated by the county, city, or state. Don't wait for an emergency.

4. Register to get free or discounted medications

Approach the pharmaceutical companies you use most to find out if they have programs for offering discounts or free medications to individuals who can meet certain qualifications. This is a service offered increasingly by leading pharmaceutical companies. You must apply to each and fill out the paperwork but the effort can be well worth it.

One program is the Partnership for Prescription Assistance: https://www.pparx.org 1-888-4PPA-NOW (1-888-477-2669)

5. Use social services

Numerous nonprofit organizations provide various types of services to individuals who are ill. Some of these programs may be right in your area. Use the internet and organizations like the United Way to find these services. You may be pleasantly surprised to find out about some of the help that is already available to you in your community.

If you're in the hospital, check to see if the hospital has a social worker on staff or can recommend a social work professional. This person will often have a vast amount of information on resources that can help patients in many ways, including programs that might provide discounts or financial assistance of some sort.

Questions to Consider

1. What are your options for health insurance coverage?
2. What advance planning can you do to make the next trip to the emergency room a better experience?
3. What agencies or governmental offices have services that can be provided to you free of charge or for reduced fees?

Journal Idea

What are the feelings and emotions you experience when you think about your experiences with physicians? Try to think of both positive and negative experiences.

Money Matters

A recent study analyzed the effect of illness on bankruptcy. Of the 2,000 participants in the study who filed bankruptcy, 50% filed for reasons related to illness. *

The presence of a serious illness creates a shock wave of problems. One of them is financial devastation. Flashing back several years, I remember one particularly nasty collection agent who called me. I'd just returned home from a long day of substitute teaching. I was pulling off my shirt when the phone rang. I answered with what little energy I had left and the person on the other end immediately attacked. He was aggressive and his tone was demeaning.

"William July?"

"Yes."

"I've been trying to call you for a month!" His voice was condescending.

"I'm Joe Nasty (name changed) from the Hassle You Inc. collection agency. Why have you been trying to avoid me? You can't avoid me anymore. I demand payment today!"

"First of all, I'm not trying to avoid you. Second, I can't pay you anything."

He cut me off and started blustering into the phone again. "Well, don't you have some relatives you can borrow the money from? A friend who will loan you the money?"

"Quite frankly, Joe, I've already tapped out loans from my family and if I were to borrow money from a friend it would be to buy medicine for my wife, not to give to you." I went on to explain to him our current health situation and the financial toll it had exacted upon us.

It was as though I'd said nothing. He continued his aggressive barrage. "Can you take out a loan to make the payment?"

I started laughing. He was trying to collect on an overdue payment and suggesting I go out and try to get a loan. It didn't even make sense.

"I must have a payment today. You can even write me a postdated check."

---

* David U. Himmelstein, Elizabeth Warren, Deborah Thorne, and Steffie Woolhandler, "Market Watch: Illness and Injury as Contributors to Bankruptcy." *Health Affairs: The Policy Journal of the Health Sphere*, February 2, 2005, W5-63, W5-71.

"That's not going to happen. In fact, let me tell you what I need you to do to help me pay off this debt. I need you to buy one of my books. Then tell each one of your friends to buy one and for them to tell a friend to buy one. If we get enough sales going, I can pay off this debt in no time. How does that sound to you?"

He didn't like my humor and ramped up his voice and started threatening me. "If you don't pay this in three days I'm going to report you to the credit bureau."

"Well, you're a little late for that. My credit score is so low now that I'm not even on the scale."

My sarcasm just made him angrier. Now it was personal to him. He wanted to show me that he was going to win this verbal joust.

"Okay, then I must inform you that my next step is to take you to court and secure a judgment against you and get it out of you that way."

I was unimpressed. "You're too late, man. We've already lost everything."

The phone was silent and then I heard a click.

I wasn't always this way with creditors. In fact, years ago, I started out by trying to explain what was going on. I also tried to work out reasonable plans to keep paying off our debts while we came out of the initial collapse caused by the illness. I wrote letters to our creditors and made minimal payments on what we could for as long as it was possible. Then, when we were no longer able to pay we wrote letters again, asking for special consideration. But only a few creditors were reasonable. The rest were even more aggressive when they found out we were financially wiped out. They didn't care, they wanted their money. I don't blame them for that. But we weren't in a position to make any payments. By this time we were on a minimal income from my substitute teaching and our remaining savings and investments were disappearing fast.

Nothing is worse than working as hard as you possibly can and putting in as many hours as you can muster the energy for, only to find out that it still isn't enough. This is the grim financial reality for many couples facing illness. Often the spouse with the illness is either unable to work or only able to work in a greatly reduced capacity. The result is a tremendous financial downshift for the couple. Suddenly bills begin to stack up; eventually even minimum payments may become impossible.

Next the creditors start calling. They call incessantly day and night. They pester, they threaten, and they hurl insults as though that would help anything. Meanwhile, I'm trying not to blow my top and go into a screaming and cursing tirade with them because my wife is asleep in the next room trying to gather up enough strength just to get up and eat her first meal of the day at 3P.M. The last thing she needs is to wake up to my worrying about something.

We Couldn't Afford to File Bankruptcy

I know it sounds odd, but we couldn't afford to file bankruptcy. Before I knew that, bankruptcy was an option I was considering. But after sitting down for an hour with a bankruptcy attorney I found out we were exactly the wrong candidates. It would have been useful for wiping out all our debts and allowing us to start over. But there was one big problem. The Chapter 7 bankruptcy which, at the time, would have virtually wiped the slate clean would not allow me to maintain the copyrights on the four books I'd written. That meant I would not receive royalty payments because I would lose my copyrights. That was out of the question. Copyrights are gold for an author. I do a lot of work on television and in the media so who knows what that can lead to. If I lost my copyrights and suddenly sold a million copies over the course of the year, I wouldn't receive one penny. That was an unacceptable risk.

Our other option was a Chapter 13 bankruptcy. This type of bankruptcy basically just reorganizes the debt, so it would have allowed us to maintain our assets, such as copyrights, while having a structured payoff. The attorney and I discussed this as the best option. But there was the small problem of our not having enough income to convince the court that we could make the negotiated payment amount. If we failed to do that, the bankruptcy would be in default and I didn't want to chance that. Basically, we couldn't afford to go bankrupt!

The last option was to slowly work our way back to financial solvency and to start rebuilding credit as soon as I secured a good regular job. Sure, couples do this every day. But there's a big difference for couples facing illness. We are paying for an illness, not an extra car, a vacation rental, a boat, or shopping sprees. It wasn't as though we were two people just working our way out of debt, needing only to cut expenses and work overtime. We were in that group of people who slipped through the cracks. My wife couldn't work and that meant I'd have to earn the equivalent of two incomes while still trying to keep pace in graduate school.

Financial Frustration

The sheer fear of not being able to provide constantly haunts the caretaker. Though you're doing your best you are always aware of the fact that you don't control all the factors that influence your ability to take care of your spouse. You don't control the economy. You don't control whether your company will merge with another. You don't control whether your company decides to move to another city, double your work load, or eliminate your position.

Perhaps nothing is more frustrating and potentially distressing for the well spouse than the heavy financial load we carry when our spouse has a debilitating illness. No matter how much I work we still have endless medical bills that aren't all covered by insurance, now that we're blessed to have insurance. Basically I have to work three times as hard as I would without the illness in our lives. First, I have to generate the income that I would normally earn. Second, I have to earn additional money to compensate for the fact that my spouse can't work. And third, I have to earn even more money to pay the bills created by the illness. And it still isn't enough!

I've spent many hours clutching a calculator and writing financial plans in a notebook, trying to map a way out of the financial pit created by the illness. I listen to some great financial experts on the radio but their advice doesn't quite fit with our situation. Financial gurus tell all of us to have three to six months of savings set aside for a rainy day. But even if you did have three to six months of income set aside, a chronic illness can deplete those reserves in a short period of time. Those calculations don't take into account long-term disability—or worse, being reduced to one income and then also having to pay out-of-pocket costs for an illness that isn't fully covered by insurance. I'd like to see a financial wizard work out a budget for a couple facing serious chronic illness on just one income with no insurance and few, if any, assets. If anyone can do that, millions of Americans would love to talk to them.

It's always funny to me when I hear the media money experts telling people to cut out their Starbucks coffee or stop spending so much on clothes, so they can save and invest more. Couples facing illness don't have that problem. Couples living with chronic illness are usually on a bare-bones survival budget. If they are fortunate enough to have any extra money, it is set aside for medical bills, healthcare, and other things not covered by insurance because they know they will have to pay major medical expenses. That's why we have to plan and budget for our individual situations. Each couple has a different set of factors to consider. With careful thought, and perhaps insights from a CPA or financial counselor who is aware of your situation, you can create a survival plan.

Like any dutiful caretaking spouse I work, work, and work more to meet our financial obligations. It's expensive to be sick, have an illness, disease, or disabling injury. The costs are staggering. It's safe to say that before the onset of the situation you didn't have this in your five-year plan. If the loss of your health (or your spouse's health) and the psychological strain, despair, and fear aren't enough, there's yet another hideous monster lurking in the shadows.

That is the monster that eats away at your personal finances. This one attacks at the core of your most basic human needs: food, clothing, and shelter and it's really mean and ugly. Prepare for battle with this monster.

Action Plan

1. Get to know your budget

Everything is radically reduced to a financial survival mode for couples facing illness. However, you still have to figure out a way to make it work. Sit down and carve out a budget strategy that you can live with. It may require you to sell your home, sell a car, work more hours, or make other sacrifices. But find a strategy that works for you. By the way, denial isn't a strategy and neither is management-by-crisis. You need a plan. Talk to a CPA or a financial planner. A professional can provide specific insights into your situation after you help them understand the details.

2. Remember that you are a team.

Make the financial aspect of your relationship a team effort. Rather than having one person taking responsibility for everything from making the income to writing the checks, find something that both partners can do in the household finance system. For example, Jamey isn't able to work now but she's a valuable bookkeeper. She sees that the bills are paid on time and has saved us money by avoiding late fees and spotting incorrect bills that I would not have caught. She makes sure we get discounts and rebates on things I'd overlook. This always adds up to a sizeable amount. She pushes herself to do what she can because as she says, when she is able to contribute in any way it makes her feel better and also gives her a vision of living a healthier life again.

Another important thing to do is to share the burden. Don't be too proud to let your spouse know how hard this is on you. They know it's tough. But when you don't tell them, it makes you feel you are facing an army alone. When you feel that way, anger, guilt, and resentment can creep in. It's better to share the pain. Even though they are ill, they want to help in whatever way they can. Sometimes all he or she can do is listen and empathize and that helps a lot. If you really feel it is too difficult for your spouse to discuss, then perhaps you should find a good therapist to talk with. You need a way to share what you are feeling. It can really relieve a lot of tension.

3. No matter what your situation is, bless it

Although bills may be draining every cent of your money, if you are actually able to pay your bills, be thankful you can do that. Be thankful that you have an income. Realize that just as things have sunk to this level, they must also get better. That's the way the universe is designed. It's balanced. This isn't some positive thinking trick. It's a spiritual principle. You want to establish the right mind-set for your life. You don't need to be in a negative mind-set because it makes you more stressed and that can only create more problems. As a practice, look for the upside of things. In your position right now, you can't afford to dwell on negative thoughts. They will consume you. On the other hand, if you look for what's good in the situation you'll start to discover opportunities that you didn't know were there.

4. Make Contact

Contact your creditors. While some will be unreasonable at least try to explain the circumstances to them. Some may work with you as long as they can. Unfortunately most creditors operate in an unreal world in which they think you have the money and just don't want to pay. But you will find a few who will give you a reprieve or reorganize your payments. It's a temporary fix at best, but it may ease the pressure.

5. Stay in Close Contact with the IRS

Contact the Internal Revenue Service and let them know of your situation. You may be surprised to hear this, but I found the IRS to be the most understanding about our problem. They worked with me from the time our debt spiraled out of control and helped us create a program that allowed us to get current on our taxes and resolve all the issues. It took some time to work through it all but I must say they were accessible, professional, and courteous.

6. Get work, any work!

Working provides at least three payoffs. First, it gives you some sort of cash flow, no matter how small. Second it allows you the feeling of actively doing something to resolve your issues. It may be only a drop in the bucket, but it will keep you from losing your mind. Third, by working, you'll unlock ideas for other employment opportunities or more income.

For example, at our lowest point when I was still working on my master's degree, I was a part-time GED instructor. This was after a failed attempt at selling fitness memberships. I was getting a very low hourly rate. But it was work. I treated that job as though I was a professor at a university. And within a few months they'd increased my pay and hours and also offered me a different full-time position. So again, positive thoughts and action yield positive results.

7. Save and invest something. Anything!

It may not be much more than a few dollars, but save and invest some money just for the energy of it. Open a separate account and put something in there each month or on some predetermined regular cycle, such as when you receive a paycheck. As your income starts to rebound you can increase the amount you save. It may not be more than a few dollars here and there but it gets you into the habit of saving and investing, and makes you conscious of the need to put money aside. If you don't have a separate savings or investment account you will lose the money in general expenses.

Again, since we are dealing with the realities of chronic illness, you may find yourself strapped for cash or needing to pay for medications or treatments. Try to allocate this out of your main budget but if you have to use some of this money you've saved, just try to avoid using it all. Don't be upset if you have to dip into that fund. Keep saving and investing so you have something there for the next emergency. Be disciplined with this extra fund and it will grow.

At the worst time during this crisis our actual investment assets totaled $14 because that was the minimum balance I could leave in my investment account to keep it open. Instead of closing the account, which would have psychologically and spiritually closed the door on that opportunity, I chose to take our every cent I could without closing it. Today, years later, our investment accounts are on a healthy rebound. Saving money is like making time. There never seems to be enough of it so you just have to make yourself do it.

Questions to Consider

1. Do you have a written budget?
2. Are there any highly expensive items in your budget you can live without?
3. Can you move to a smaller home or drive a less expensive car?
4. Have you attempted to contact those to whom you are in debt?

Journal Idea

How does money affect your marriage? Write about how you and your spouse can make the financial aspect of your marriage healthy.

The Platitudes
(and my not-so-gracious responses)

As you read this, please note that none of this is to say I don't appreciate the sympathy and well wishes of people, because I do. I also understand some people may say the following things just because they are at a loss for words. I accept that. A kind word is the water a parched spirit needs in order to last one more moment. But there's a fine line between authentic sympathy and someone just tossing you a bone of platitudes to chew on.

Forgive me if I sound ungrateful but we've lost a dream home, two cars, three dogs, savings, investments, dreams, and plans. I've watched my wife's body go from a petite model of fitness to being distorted and distended with illness. I've suffered through watching her endure a second wave of devastation from the medications prescribed by several doctors. I'm sure you can understand why I'm not in the mood to hear another platitude delivered with a pat on the back. I'm much more interested in action.

Here's a list of clichés every chronically ill person and their spouse are tired of hearing. I'm not sure why people feed us this stuff but I think they say these things for several reasons. Often they don't know what to say. The situation is so horrible that it scares them and they default to a list of clichés like emotional robots. Some people don't want to be bothered by you and the illness, the same way they don't want the homeless guy on the corner coming up to their car, so they shooh you away with a platitude. It makes them feel magnanimous, as though they've done something great to help you.

I grew up with parents who suffered from chronic illness and now I have a wife who has been hit with a severe chronic illness. Through it all I've had to learn how to live in tandem with chronic illness. It's not a simple process but it can be done. However, you won't find any answers in platitudes. I promise we won't deliver a bunch of platitudes in this book. If you're taking the time to read this book, you're probably so deep in the experience of supporting a spouse or facing illness yourself that you are making time to read it. I intend to make this investment of your time worthwhile. So you won't ever hear me say …

1. "Hang in there."
   Obviously you're hanging in there. If you weren't you wouldn't be surviving even as well as you are now, even if you're only making it moment to moment. You don't need anyone to tell you that.

2. "You've got to be strong."
   No kidding!

3. "I admire you. I don't see how you do it."
   I don't really need admiration, I need help.

4. "Just keep praying."
   I am praying. But I have to take action too. God isn't a fast-food drive-through where you place a prayer order and the answer pops out ready to go.

5. "I'll pray for you."
   Praying for us is great. But could you also put some of that prayer into the form of some assistance? For example, while I'm at work my wife could use a ride to the doctor, Thursday. Oh, you're busy that day? Okay, sorry to bother you.

6. "Things will get better."
   Actually, things may or may not get better. Chronic illness isn't like catching a cold. It doesn't usually just go away. Most of us will have to make permanent changes in our lives and family systems.

7. "I feel sorry for you."
   Well, thank you very much. I appreciate that and I feel better now.

8. "What doesn't kill you will make you stronger."
   Not the best words for people in a life-and-death struggle.

9. "It could always be worse."
   Yes, that's true. In fact this is one platitude that I actually find some comfort in. However, sometimes things are pretty bad so I don't spend much time thinking about how much worse it could be. It also backfires in that it makes me think about these people are who really are worse off than me. How is that going to make me feel better?
   If you're tired of hearing this type of platitude or cliché advice you've come to the right place. The following pages talk frankly about the devastation of chronic illness on a middle-class family. And, more importantly, what you can do in the face of this so everyone involved can have a life beyond illness.

Action Plan

1. Realize Everyone Is Different

One thing that has helped me endure platitudes from people is remembering that everyone thinks differently. I try to envision things from their point of view. I mentioned earlier how this might be their best effort. Sure, some people are just being robots but others are sincere and they may not be able to say something original or inspiring. It doesn't necessarily mean they are trying to dismiss the seriousness of the situation.

2. Don't Edit

When someone tries to comfort you they may not say what you want to hear, or the way you want it said. Avoid editing what they say because you are responding from a raw and painful place. Your response could easily make you turn into a fire-breathing dragon and you will scorch a person who was well intentioned, albeit not very well spoken or eloquent. There's a learned art to listening to what others say without judgment or interruption and this is a good time to develop and use that skill.

3. Give Permission for Silence

Give people permission not to say anything at all. This option is good when words aren't enough. Sometimes people feel pressured to say something or do something. We can eliminate that by telling them up front that we appreciate their concern and presence and that they don't need to feel they have to say or do something profound to make us feel better.

Questions to Consider

1. What platitudes do you hear most often?
2. How can you discern whether a platitude is sincere or not?
3. What do you tell people when you are comforting them?

Journal Idea

What is something you'd like to have someone say to you?

The Critics

Everyone is not emotionally and psychologically equipped to handle close interaction with a person suffering from a severe illness. Hearing a friend or loved one sobbing, watching their body deteriorate, and witnessing them go through medieval looking medical procedures is more than some can bear.

A close relative of my wife is an example. I think she just couldn't handle the situation. The first time she heard Jamey crying and describing her illness she became angry. She quizzed Jamey about ways she might be causing the illness herself. She suggested it was all in her head. She accused her of just wanting to get attention. She even went a step further. She called one day and when I answered the phone she immediately launched into a rage implying that I wasn't doing a good job helping my wife get well.

This is something the spouse of a chronically ill person never wants to hear. You already know you're doing all you can and then someone outside of the situation has the audacity to sit back and judge your performance. I wasn't happy about this and we exchanged words. She was yelling as she told me how doctors could help Jamey and I must not be taking her to the right specialists. She continued her rant by suggesting ideas and solutions that we'd already tried. Finally, after I continued to object to her ideas she yelled, "Well, if there's no other alternative then just put her in an institution on a morphine drip!"

That blew me away on several levels. First, it reminded me of how much blind faith some people put in the medical profession because they need to believe there's an answer that a doctor can pull out of a magic medical book. On the larger level, I thought about all of the people who are actually institutionalized because their families just threw their hands up in frustration. I thought about all of the people who'd probably been misdiagnosed with mental disorders because they had an odd disease. It was a sad and sobering thought.

Why Some People React This Way

To gain more insight on this we have to look at a basic principle of human behavior. It's very difficult for most people to understand something they have no experience with. Before many people will accept something they don't understand, their first tendency is to disagree, deny, or doubt, especially if it's a complicated or uncomfortable issue. That's why even after you tell some of your family members and friends what you are going through, they may not understand it. Don't expect them to understand. In fact, I recommend that you are very careful about disclosing your situation. Don't tell too many people what you're going through. Many just won't get it and they may even dismiss you and your spouse as quacks. Remember, as I said previously, if your spouse is dealing with an illness that is unknown, you're on your own except for people who are highly empathetic and others who find themselves in that same predicament. Therefore, you can expect a lot of people to be clueless about what you're going through.

There are basically three ways most people will respond your spouse's illness:

1. Denial—When the situation is too stark or ugly some people pretend it isn't happening. They treat it lightly by glossing over it and minimizing the severity.

2. Criticizing—Some people try to handle the situation by criticizing. These people will often blame the ill person for their condition. This provides them with what they feel is a logical explanation and control over the situation. This helps them to manage emotionally.

3. The blank faced stare—This is what you get from people who are totally clueless. They don't have a module plugged in to understand the situation. They don't get where you're coming from. They register that it is a sad situation, but they don't know what to do or say so they don't say or do anything. On the phone this can be heard in a thick, long, and palpable silence.

Again, it's important to keep in mind that when people don't respond in the way that you think they should, remember that what you're experiencing isn't the script that most people are living. Therefore they usually just don't get it. So don't judge them too quickly as being cold and removed. However, if you want them to understand, you'll have to learn how to explain what you're going through to them in terms they can grasp. After you've told them in a way they understand, then you can determine whether or not they seem to care.

Action Plan

1. Don't play head games with the critics

The critics can be powerful influences on your emotions because their doubts shake up your fears and concerns. Your best defense against critics is to mentally dismiss them or to avoid them. You don't have to be rude. Just don't participate in their mind games. Realize that you're living the experience and they are only providing an editorial opinion from their perch in life. Some people only understand what they've experienced themselves. From there they often attempt to generalize about others, but what they imagine is often off target.

2. Create and maintain boundaries

Critics need boundaries. They thrive on negativity and that is exactly what you don't need. Take control and set the tone in conversations with them. Steer away from your sensitive topics. If that can't be accomplished, politely and calmly end the conversation.

Questions to Consider

1. Who are your critics?
2. What is the emotional response you have when you encounter your critics?
3. How can you minimize your emotional response to the critics?

Journal Idea

Write a letter in your journal to your biggest critic. In this letter, let the person know how you feel about their behavior.

Is Your Doctor Hazardous to Your Health?

The following incidents are some snapshots of our experiences with the health-care system during this illness. Because this is our actual experience and so many others can empathize and sympathize with this, I would be remiss to edit or omit it just for the sake of fearing to sound too critical toward the specific physicians mentioned in this chapter. To do so would be untrue to the purpose of this book, which is to provide empathy, information, and inspiration, to those who are facing life with chronic illness. It is not my intention to malign MDs. I respect anyone who endures the obstacle course necessary in obtaining any sort of doctoral level degree. I personally know the sacrifice involved in achieving the doctoral level. Furthermore, I have friends and colleagues who are MDs. But none of that changes what Jamey and I experienced. This chapter is a story echoed by far too many people who are trying to live with chronic illnesses, especially those who are dealing with invisible chronic illnesses (undiagnosed illnesses, rare diseases, or newly evolving conditions).

The Medical Deity (a.k.a., The Grinch)

Jamey's appointment was just around the corner from our home. But the problem was that she was too weak to drive herself and nobody else was available to take her. I was making a sprint from the campus in West Houston through the early afternoon traffic to get home and take her to the doctor. This was an important one and we couldn't reschedule. We had an appointment with a highly recommended infectious disease specialist to whom a physician we trusted had referred us. She'd already told us that the specialist was doing her a favor by working us in on short notice. She'd examined Jamey a week earlier and seen the severity of her symptoms. However, it was outside her area of expertise. I was optimistic despite having seen so many doctors, only to have my enthusiasm fizzle out when I saw the bewildered look in their eyes or heard their empty explanations that I could tell even they didn't believe.

His office was ordinary enough. It was small and nondescript. Jamey was told he was ready and my mother and I accompanied her to the exam room. I always go to the first meeting or two with a new physician; if I can't, I ask my mother to go since she is a retired registered nurse. I've found it makes a big difference in the way a person is treated when the physician knows the family is involved. Also, it helps when I'm there because I can help Jamey explain the situation.

We waited for about ten minutes and then in he walked. Or, should I say, descended down to our mere mortal level. He was a gangly man who walked awkwardly. He had long, skinny arms and legs, a thin frame, and a potbelly that gave him an even stranger appearance. In fact, he looked a lot like the Grinch from *The Grinch Who Stole Christmas*. He contemptuously surveyed us through his bifocals as though we were serfs who'd been summoned before the king.

Folding his hands together, he sank back into his seat as though meditating. He didn't really make eye contact, just sort of stared near Jamey. He proceeded to speak in measured tones. This man clearly felt his words were weighty and that he was profound, if only to himself.

Odd character, I remember thinking. I figured perhaps he was just eccentric. But I should've known something was wrong when his line of questioning veered off course. Noting that Jamey's eyes were watery and that she was using a Kleenex, he asked her if she had a cold. She tried to explain to him that she had been experiencing ongoing allergic reactions since her initial symptoms started, but this doctor held up his hand signaling for her to stop talking, and began to inform her that she was not answering him properly. He continued to carry out this method of asking my wife questions about her symptoms and experience and then abruptly interrupting her reply before she could finish. He would intersperse his questions to Jamey with random questions unrelated to her illness and the purpose of the consultation. Then he turned to me and started asking me what I did for a living. When he found out I was a psychologist his demeanor changed a little. But then he started telling me everything about psychology. He obviously felt he was an expert on every subject.

Okay, I thought. I'll play along because if he's really such an esteemed expert maybe he can help her and this will just be something we look back on and laugh about. The referring physician had warned us that he was eccentric, but she had said he was reputed to be a top infectious disease doctor. Yet this man wasn't getting anywhere. He was careening further and further into outer space and taking us along for the ride. Finally, he began to focus more on questions about Jamey's symptoms. We typically show a new doctor pictures of Jamey before her illness so they can have a frame of reference for the toll the illness has taken, as well as some photos of her since her condition has progressed, that depict some of her physical symptoms. He summarily dismissed all of the photos we showed him except one. For some reason he zoomed in on a photo of Jamey and her grandmother, Lucille, who at that time was in her late 80s and in a wheelchair.

"Who's the fat lady?" he said, without moving from his pious position.

Jamey, my mother, and I were in shock. I thought I was hearing things.

Jamey shot back, "That's my grandmother and she'd be very hurt by your comment."

Any normal person would've known that was enough. But not this guy. Before he examined my wife, he had made the startling proclamation that he could tell from simply looking at her, that she did not have the conditions that we were seeing him for. When he proceeded to examine Jamey, he merely looked at her eyes and throat and a rash on her arm. Jamey and my mom explained that she had some very pronounced places on her skin in the back and chest area that he should see. They tried to get him to look at the extreme indentions that her socks had made to show how much edema my wife was experiencing. However, he waved their suggestions aside and announced that the so-called exam was over. Then he declared, "You've just gone and gotten fat."

Okay, now I wanted to punch him. I was furious. He wouldn't look at the indentations that could be easily made in my wife's skin which were quite unusual, or at the series of photos over the years showing her in excellent physical shape, and he could, like some demigod, determine that she did not have certain diseases simply from looking at her? In fact, just a few days later, we were able to see another specialist in the same field who not only examined my wife from head to toe, noting "severe pit edema" and the numerous skin irregularities but also ordered several blood tests. From the examination and extensive blood work, this physician told us that Jamey did indeed have the conditions we had suspected. These were the same conditions the grinch had said she didn't have.

He wasn't getting any more of our time. We all got up and started for the door. But he wasn't finished. He kept talking. He started lecturing us about how doctors are rational people of science … blah … blah … I thought to myself, is he crazy? He's lecturing someone with a Ph.D. in psychology about scientific thinking? By the time I finished that thought we were all out of the door.

Some people reading this might say, why didn't we just leave earlier and tell him a thing or two on the way out? Well, it's not that simple when you can't find anyone with answers and your loved one is in pain constantly. You can feel desperate sometimes. Of course, in hindsight I wish we'd left earlier. I think I was so desperate that I hoped, even though he was a pontificating eccentric, he might have something worthwhile to say underneath it all. But he didn't. It was not only a waste of time but also demoralizing. I fought the colossal Houston traffic to make it back in time to teach my evening class. We learned a lot that day and we have handled things very differently since.

The Sleepy Surgeon

The sleepy surgeon, as we later called him, met us for an appointment early in the evening. He came into the room in a hurry, clearly rushed, and was out of breath from getting to our appointment on time. His lab coat was disheveled, his blond hair was rumpled, and his black cowboy boots looked as though they hadn't ever known the pleasure of a good shine. He was a big guy, slightly over-weight, and young. The sleepy surgeon had agreed to work with us to see if the severe pain in Jamey's right pelvic/groin area was from a hernia. He had taken more than a week to look over the CAT scan and had allegedly engaged three other associates to assist in examining the film. He concluded that Jamey did have a small hernia in the right groin area and suggested surgery to correct it, but said he would have to call us to let us know when he could work her into his busy schedule.

Noticing how stressed and tired this man seemed I couldn't help but ask him about it. I matter-of-factly said to him, "You look tired."

He looked back at me quickly and nodded. "I am. I've been working 12 hours straight all week."

"Are you doing that much surgery?"

"Yea, I'm going to leave here and go back to do another one this evening."

"Wow, man. When do you rest?"

"I don't," he said, shaking his head. He seemed relieved that someone had acknowledged his exhaustion.

"Dude, you need to get some rest. There will be plenty of people to cut on later," I said as he left the room.

He laughed. As the door closed I looked at Jamey and cringed.

That was Thursday evening. The next evening his office called around seven o'clock to let my wife know they had a sudden opening for surgery on Monday morning at seven thirty. They needed to know right away if we were going to take that slot so they could schedule the surgery. Jamey and I both have made it a practice throughout her experience with this illness not to rush into any pro-cedure—especially after what she had been through with the ER and hospital fiasco a year and a half earlier. She told the doctor's office manager that we'd have to get back with her but the woman said she needed an answer right away. Jamey held her hand over the phone and asked me what I thought. I immedi-ately said, "No way. We're not rushing into surgery with your fragile condition and especially with that guy." Jamey said she had said an inner prayer for guidance as she was talking with the doctor's office manager and immediately felt that she should not take the surgical appointment. The woman on the phone seemed perturbed but Jamey just told her that since it was already the weekend, we'd not have time to get approval from our insurance provider for the early surgery, and that I would not have time to get a substitute professor to teach my morning class at the university. She told Jamey that she could not say when the next opening would be.

That turned out to be the best decision we could have made. As the pain in her right groin and pelvic area seemed to worsen, the next week Jamey went to an independent diagnostic X-ray clinic. The clinic ran a routine X-ray on her right pelvic area. After the test was done Jamey and my mom saw a nurse-technician approaching them. Clearly something was bothering her. She told Jamey and my mom that they would have to let the physician who was in charge of reading the X-ray call us with the results. Then she turned and delicately whispered to my wife, "I'm not supposed to tell you this, but no one can prevent you from opening this copy of your X-ray and seeing that you have a broken hip!" Reaching for a wheelchair, she told my wife to sit in it and to try to stay off the hip until a physician could advise her further. She then turned again and in a low voice asked, "Did your doctor mention anything about the broken bones?" My wife was so stunned at this information, she just shook her head, "No."

To sum it all up the sleepy surgeon had not only taken more than a week to read my wife's CAT scan along with the purported assistance of three additional doctors, but he and these other doctors had also overlooked the two obvious fractures in Jamey's right pelvic area. Upon seeing an orthopedic specialist a week later, we were shown on the CAT scan where the fractures were obvious even to the untrained eye in virtually every frame of the film! We learned that fractures of this sort would typically occur from a high-impact car crash or a fall from a four-or five-story building, but in Jamey's case (since no accident or incident had occurred) they were considered to be "spontaneous fractures" due to the fact that her bones had become very brittle. It was only at that time we discovered that she had developed osteoporosis—a side effect of the medication that she had been put on during her hospital nightmare.

All that pain was coming from the fractures in her hip that the sleepy surgeon (and his colleagues) had not even noticed. In fact, he was going to operate on her for a small hernia in her groin without any knowledge or concern for those broken pelvic bones! We thank God to this day that we refused to rush into that operation as there is no telling what sort of extensive damage may have occurred under the circumstances.

The Pathologist Who Thought He Was a Psychologist

During the first year of experiencing this chronic condition, my wife saw a well-respected pathologist who examined her for all of about 30 seconds and told her the problem was all in her head. Then he proceeded to tell her a cautionary tale about another of his patients whose life was ruined because he was imagining that he was having the same symptoms.

Here's the irony of it all. We would later see another well-respected specialist who would send my wife's biopsy samples to this same pathologist for examination. Wouldn't you know that upon appeal from another physician and not knowing it was my wife's tissue he was testing, this same pathologist actually did find a pathological issue present in the sample from my wife.

The Patronizer

Last but not least there was another physician who examined Jamey early in the onset of her illness and said he didn't see anything wrong with her. He summed it up by saying, "You're such a pretty little lady. I hate to see you going through all of this. Why don't you just go home and enjoy your life"!

The Reality of Being Sick

Navigating the sick care system isn't easy. We want to believe that when we get sick we merely need to go to the doctor and there will be a pill, procedure, or surgery that will fix everything. But it's not that simple with chronic illness.

What's interesting to me is that scientific thinking in its purest sense is about inquiry. As a psychologist I was trained rigorously in scientific methodology. But I still see at the root of any new theory or scientific proposition that the source has to be a new idea. At some point somebody has to think of something new and try it. For the most part, I haven't found this to be true with the physicians we've seen. Most are content to be MDs (medicine dispensers) but it doesn't seem there's a lot of the practice of medicine going on.

Well-intentioned people often ask the obvious question: have you taken her to the doctor? Often I want to give a sarcastic answer. But I realize people are well meaning and it's a perfectly understandable question from someone unfamiliar with chronic illness. After finding out a little about our odyssey within the sick-care system, they will offer some advice: what you need is a good specialist. Depending upon what mood I'm in I thank them courteously or nod in agreement and say, "We've been to the best." But what I really want to tell them is that their faith in doctors and the health-care system is naïve. In reality, it seems once you go beyond a broken arm, heart attack, or cancer, you're on your own. Such is the world of chronic illness. The health-care system simply doesn't know what to do with these people.

Finding the right care provider for a chronic illness isn't as simple as looking on your HMO or PPO plan and finding a name. Unfortunately it isn't even as simple as getting a referral. Chronic illness is like floating on a vast sea of mystery. Each wave is some unexplained symptom or phenomenon that is all too real to those experiencing it, yet bizarre or outrageous sounding to someone working within the confines of a sick-care system.

For the chronically ill and their spouses the first stop is the doctor. After all, that's what we've all grown up believing—the idea that the doctor will heal you. In sociology there's a theory known as the sick role. An inherent part of the sick role is the expertise of the doctor and the vulnerability and need of the patient. This is the foundation of the medical model. The patient is sick and the doctor is the healer. This is instilled in doctors during training, and this mentality is part of a culture that pervades the entire medical system. This is where the joke about MD meaning "medical deity" comes from. This philosophy isn't really a problem for most people because their transactions with a doctor are rather limited and temporary. They have a minor or traditional illness for which they go to the doctor and receive medication or a surgical procedure or both, that is more or less the extent of their relationship until the next time.

However, for the millions of people dealing with chronic conditions, the relationship with medical doctors can be very challenging in and of itself. The person with a chronic condition is ill and often the doctor can't figure it out or, if he or she can identify the illness, they often have very limited knowledge or resources for effective treatments. Nothing is more deflating than seeing a highly recommended specialist at a major research institution furrow his brow and say, "I have no idea what this is." We've found that when you're floating on the vast sea of unexplained chronic illness you will get four responses from the health-care system:

1. Prescriptions that don't address the actual problem (and may even exacerbate the patient's condition because of the additional side effects that many of these drugs incite).

2. Empty referrals from doctor to doctor.

3. Being told it's all in your mind (usually by doctors who have little or no knowledge in the practice of psychology and have not seen the patient enough to even come to such a conclusion).

4. Then there's the rare blunt honesty: "You're clearly ill with something but I don't know what it is."

One doctor was so baffled by my wife's symptoms that he got angry. He initially told her she needed to "live in a bubble," referring to her challenged immune system. But he was apparently so frustrated by the physical symptoms he was seeing and not knowing what she had or how to treat it that he asked her to leave and said he would not charge her for the visit. Remember, doctors and surgeons are people. That means that a good number of them, as with any other group of people, have personal issues, fears, and a limit to their knowledge. This would not pose nearly as many problems for patients if these medical professionals would be honest in their evaluation and assessment. In other words, if they don't know the condition, say that. If they don't know how to treat a condition, admit it. This would be far more constructive than attempting to make the patient feel that they are delusional, or dispensing medications that are not going to alleviate the symptoms or cure the illness.

Action Plan

1. Be an advocate for your spouse

Advocating for your spouse includes, among other things, going with them to the doctor. Of course, you may not be able to make every appointment. But try to be there for the first appointment with a new doctor. The chronically ill can be understandably defeated, angry, or too compliant with doctors. Your presence allows them to have a person there who is close to the situation to monitor and provide input and explanations when necessary, somewhat like a good coach who stands on the sidelines guiding and supporting the athlete on the field. Also, it helps your situation a lot when the physician sees that the patient has family support. Although this shouldn't matter, it does. In addition, it generally causes a service provider to increase their performance a notch because they're being observed.

2. Don't just rely on what the doctor tells you

Use the internet to gather information on the conditions, and to research everything the doctor tells you. It has a wealth of information on almost anything imaginable. With a number of websites available to explain medical conditions, illnesses, drugs, and treatments. If you invest some time you can find information from experts, pharmaceutical manufacturers, researchers, patients' firsthand accounts, and support groups.

3. Don't expect a doctor to be God

Doctors are only human. No more and no less. They can't just write out a prescription or carry out a surgical procedure to fix any and everything. Realize the limitations of a doctor when going to see them. Expect them to help you within the scope of their knowledge and skill. Realigning your focus in this way causes you to become accountable with your spouse for finding relief and solutions for the problem. This is where your doctor becomes a member of your team instead of the sole focus of the healing solution. It is a critical shift that can transform how you feel about the experience. And remember, a doctor should never tell you that you can't be healed. They can only say their ability to heal you has ceased and you need to go to someone else.

4. Look outside the box

One of the major issues with chronic health conditions is that protocols for cures or effective treatments are almost nonexistent. As discussed previously, conventional medicine is left scratching its head about many of these conditions. Some people have found relief of symptoms through alternative methods. Treatment plans prescribed by osteopathic doctors, chiropractors, acupuncturists, herbalists, and innovative therapies such as hyperbaric oxygen therapy, ultraviolet light for skin and immunities, ultraviolet blood irradiation, and natural cell therapy may be alternatives to investigate. Adding these practitioners to our care team has been a beneficial experience for us. If you search the internet for proof of efficacy of these methods you will find it is a split decision in many cases. There is empirical evidence to argue both for against alternative approaches. Which again, points to the fact that the ultimate choice and decisions must be made by you, and your spouse, demonstrating the necessity of being as well informed as you can.

5. Assemble a care-provider team

If you're fortunate you'll eventually assemble a dream team. But if not, you'll still need a reliable doctor. One who listens, doesn't think you're crazy, and isn't afraid to think outside the box. This is no overnight task but it must be done. You need a team of medical doctors—not medical deities, medical doubters, or medicine dispensers. Ask doctors you respect for referrals to other doctors like them. If you meet a doctor and you don't think he or she is appropriate for you, keep looking. As with any other profession, there are some excellent physicians out there and there are others who shouldn't have a license. Always check the credentials of the physician. In our state, Texas, this is easy because the Texas Medical Board has a website in which entering the physicians name will yield complete information about their education and any disciplinary actions they've received.

Our team consists of an MD who works with traditional, alternative, and holistic treatments; a dermatologist who is also a researching microbiologist; an acupuncturist who also works with herbs; a deep tissue massage therapist; and an expert compounding pharmacist. This team has been able to provide us with some of the health-care resources we need.

Questions to Consider

1. Have you researched the diagnoses and medications you have?
2. Are you and your primary physician able to communicate openly and with mutual respect?
3. Have you met your spouse's physicians?

Journal Idea

What experiences have you had with physicians? Why is it important to have your spouse, family, and medical professionals understand your illness?

Don't Let Them Kill You
with the Cure

Ironically, on a trip back home to Houston to see a specialist, Jamey's health took a critical turn for the worse. We'd gone to Houston to see a respected specialist at Baylor College of Medicine. When this physician examined Jamey two years prior to this visit, he had determined that she didn't have anything wrong. However, now he was clearly baffled at the rashes and little marks that looked like insect bites all over her body, as well as at how much her muscles had atrophied since her last visit. He told her he'd never seen anything like her condition and highly recommended she see one of his colleagues while we were in Houston.

That night at the hotel she was having trouble sleeping and her body began to swell mysteriously. Hour by hour, the swelling increased. Soon she was so swollen she could hardly breathe. I was in the other room of our suite watching a rebroadcast of a football game when she called me into the room. I'd been monitoring her swelling but it had really become critical since the last time I looked in on her. It was another bizarre episode of this illness. Around 3 a.m. we called an ambulance. At this time we still had no insurance although we were supposed to be insured through the COBRA benefits from my former job. However, they denied coverage upon our attempting to sign into the emergency room. But that's another story. Jamey was admitted to the hospital because her condition had become life threatening—something was going terribly wrong in her body. Unknown to us, this trip to the emergency room would eventually result in more years of suffering for her because of the medication she would receive.

Jamey was admitted to a room and appointed a hospital internist to oversee her treatment. To arrest the swelling this physician decided it was necessary to give Jamey massive intravenous doses of prednisone. Our attorney would later tell us that the amount she received was in excess of the manufacturer's recommended maximum dosage. The problem is that once started, this drug has to be tapered down slowly or it can cause devastating health complications or death. We were in a bad situation. She was given the huge dosage which meant she'd have to taper down from it over time. This meant she would have a dangerous level of this drug in her system for longer than recommended. Prednisone can have very serious side effects if it is taken in large doses over a period of time. Making matters worse, over the next few months we learned that tapering off from prednisone was not easy for some patients. Jamey was having a very difficult time and no physicians we consulted seemed to have an answer, other than to keep trying and to go to the emergency room if the side effects became life threatening.

The so-called side effects Jamey has suffered have become so severe we now have two monsters to fight: the illness and the treatment! Here's a list of side effects she experienced that are directly attributed to the medication she was given:

1. Sudden weight gain and severe pit edema (overall swelling)
2. High blood pressure
3. Inability to fight infections
4. Osteoporosis
5. Bone necrosis and multiple spontaneous fractures (bones breaking without any impact or injury to the body)
6. Easy bruising and slow healing of cuts on the skin
7. Cataracts and subsequent surgery to correct the condition
8. Insomnia, bouts of depression, and mood swings*
9. Heart palpitations, chest pains and at least one minor heart attack

The Lawsuit that Never Happened

Outraged, we wanted to sue. Sure you can sue. But let's face the facts about lawsuits. They're long, tedious, expensive, and emotionally draining. Moreover, you have to find a lawyer with the guts to follow through on a suit against a doctor, hospital, or insurer. Not many of them want to get into that kind of gutter brawl in these days of tort reform and stricter guidelines with smaller settlements. We had to work hard to find a lawyer willing to take our case. I always wonder where the people who file frivolous lawsuits find attorneys. How do they find lawyers while people with legitimate cases can't?

When we tried to get a lawyer for our legitimate case it was like pulling teeth. It was as though we were on trial during their interviews with us. Of course I

---

* "Treatments: Prednisone," The Johns Hopkins Vasculitis Center (2006), http://vasculitis.med.jhu.edu/treatments/prednisone.html

understand the need for lawyers to vet a case to discover potential snares and to weed out fraudulent or capricious clients. But the real problem stems from tort reforms that restrict individuals with valid cases to having a cap (typically $250,000) on what can be awarded to the victim. In states such as Texas it is now almost impossible to get any justice or compensation for citizens who have legitimately suffered undue loss through medical negligence or malpractice. Some may think $250,000 is a lot of money but when you take out 33-40 percent for the attorney's fees, then subtract court fees, that leaves a paltry sum. That's when and if you survive the long and arduous odyssey to actually winning a settlement, which is money needed for paying recurring healthcare expenses, food, clothing, and shelter, not to buy a new Mercedes! On the other hand, we have cases such as the Washington D.C. judge who, representing himself, dragged a dry cleaner into court to sue them for $54 million dollars over a pair of lost pants.* Something is wrong with this picture.

We finally found a good lawyer who agreed to take the case despite some reluctance due to the tort reform legislation. He told us there was a chance for a minimal settlement, which he would pursue, but that we should not get too hopeful about it. Under tort reform our ability to sue was greatly restricted and the amount we could recover was significantly limited. It was like rubbing salt into a wound when he told us that a few years earlier he could have won a multimillion dollar settlement for something like this.

I'll fast forward to the eleventh hour. The statute of limitations was about to run out on us. The attorney had advised us to file immediately if we were going to go through with the case. Late the night before the deadline we were sorting through papers, making copies, and assembling files. Honestly, with what we'd been told and all that we were already going through, I wasn't highly motivated for this. I looked over at Jamey. She was weak and swollen from the medication, with only enough energy to look through the files and make copies for 10 minutes. How was she going to sustain a long and hostile legal battle?

Also, I thought about the psychological toll. If we engaged in a suit we'd be engaged in the process for years. I just didn't see how it could be a healthy way of living under the circumstances. We were already trying to overcome the dejection from the illness. The suit would force us to focus on the problems, to meditate on them, and to relive them over and over. I looked at Jamey and said, "I'll support you if you want to go through with this … but I don't want to do it. I think it will be harder on us than whatever it will be worth."

She was relieved. Without hesitation she agreed. No ifs, ands, or buts. We stopped right then and there, boxed up the papers, and went on with our lives,

---

* Associated Press, June 13, 2007 7:52PM, CST

uncertain what could have happened but definitely not carrying the stress of a long lawsuit that might not have netted us anything substantial for paying medical bills. I'm not suggesting that everyone do that. But it was what was best for us. It was as though we were playing "Deal or No Deal" and deciding not to pursue the lawsuit was our way of pressing the button and getting peace of mind. The price we'd have had to pay just to try was too high.

Action Plan

1. Be proactive

If you are the well spouse and your spouse is receiving treatment in a hospital, try to be there during the treatment. Your presence increases the sense of accountability the doctor has. When Jamey was administered the "killer cure" medication, I wasn't present because I had to be back at my job in another city. Had I been able to stay and talk with the physician I may have been able to help Jamey dissuade him from administering that medication, or at least get him to try a lower dosage.

Before treatment or procedures begin, discuss your spouse's health history and condition with the doctor. Make sure he or she knows what's going on. Many of them will welcome this although some may seem irritated by your presence. But that's okay, they don't have to live with the results. Be sure you understand what the doctor is going to do. They should be able to explain it to you in plain English.

While your spouse is in the hospital, visit regularly. If you can't be there, make sure a friend or relative can go in your place. Make sure the nursing staff knows you and knows how to contact you. Give them your cell phone number or a work number. Make personal contact. Don't let your spouse be seen as just another patient in a room. Treat the nurses well because they work very hard and are usually under staffed and under paid. Like anyone else, they are kind to those who treat them with dignity.

2. Explore non-invasive and minimally invasive options to procedures and surgeries

Today, everything doesn't require the same invasive techniques as in the past. Discuss alternatives to surgery and invasive treatments with your doctor. There may be options. I remember how a surgeon once suggested I have a somewhat invasive procedure when I had an infection that caused a sac of fluid to collect around my heart. The surgeon suggested he drain it in a procedure utilizing a long needle. It sounded a bit medieval to me and made me wince. When I asked about other alternatives, he said there was a drug we could try. The drug cleared up the excess fluid in my chest and I avoided the invasive technique that would have involved inherently higher risks to my health. But had I not asked he would not have proposed the less invasive option.

3. Know your rights as a patient*

In November 1997, President Clinton's Advisory Commission on Consumer Protection and Quality on the Health Care Industry, in an Interim Report, issued the Patients' Bill of Rights and Responsibilities.

1. *The Right to Information*
Patients have the right to receive accurate, easily understood information to assist them in making informed decisions about their health plans, facilities and professionals.

2. *The Right to Choose*
Patients have the right to a choice of health care providers that is sufficient to assure access to appropriate high-quality health care including giving women access to qualified specialists such as obstetrician-gynecologists and giving patients with serious medical conditions and chronic illnesses access to specialists.

3. *Access to Emergency Services*
Patients have the right to access emergency health services when and where the need arises. Health plans should provide payment when a patient presents himself/herself to any emergency department with acute symptoms of sufficient severity "including severe pain" that a "prudent layperson" could reasonably expect the absence of medical attention to result in placing that consumer's health in serious jeopardy, serious impairment to bodily functions, or serious dysfunction of any bodily organ or part.

4. *Being a Full Partner in Health Care Decisions*
Patients have the right to fully participate in all decisions related to their health care. Consumers who are unable to fully participate in treatment decisions have the right to be represented by parents, guardians, family members, or other conservators. Additionally, provider contracts should not contain any so-called "gag clauses" that restrict health professionals' ability to discuss and advise patients on medically necessary treatment options.

5. *Care Without Discrimination*
Patients have the right to considerate, respectful care from all members of the health care industry at all times and under all circumstances. Patients must not be discriminated against in the marketing or enrollment or in the provision of

---

* This entire section is excerpted from "The Patients' Bill of Rights in Medicare and Medicaid," United States Department of Health and Human Services Fact Sheet (April 12, 1999), http://www.hhs.gov/news/press/1999pres/990412.html

health care services, consistent with the benefits covered in their policy and/or as required by law, based on race, ethnicity, national origin, religion, sex, age, current or anticipated mental or physical disability, sexual orientation, genetic information, or source of payment.

6. *The Right to Privacy*
Patients have the right to communicate with health care providers in confidence and to have the confidentiality of their individually-identifiable health care information protected. Patients also have the right to review and copy their own medical records and request amendments to their records.

7. *The Right to Speedy Complaint Resolution*
Patients have the right to a fair and efficient process for resolving differences with their health plans, health care providers, and the institutions that serve them, including a rigorous system of internal review and an independent system of external review.

8. *Taking on New Responsibilities*
In a health care system that affords patients rights and protections, patients must also take greater responsibility for maintaining good health.

Questions to Consider

1. Do you ask your physician about alternatives to invasive procedures?
2. What are the potential side effects of your medications? Are there potential dangers in mixing any of your medications?
3. Are you aware of your rights as a patient?

Journal Idea

Do you know when it's best to fight something and when it's best to let it go? How does your health factor into that decision?

Her Tears in the Night

It was late afternoon on a sweltering Texas summer day in Austin. The sun was beaming down from a cloudless sky. A hot breeze crossed my path as I headed up the walk toward the front door. Inside, the cool air hit me and I breathed a sigh of relief. I leaned back against the door and enjoyed the peaceful silence of our living room. It was good to be home.

No sooner had my thoughts of relaxation set in than I began to tense up. There was no visible cause for alarm. No sign of anything to panic about. But this had become my ritual. A little panic would set in as I returned home each day because I never knew what I'd find. Sometimes it would hit me in the car as I drove home. Sometimes it would start when I walked in the door.

It wasn't all unfounded. Some days when I left for work Jamey would be asleep with a stiff and pained-looking face. Looking at that mask—the result of the illness and the medications—was a difficult sight. There were times when I really wondered if I'd get a call from the emergency room telling me my wife had called 911 and that the paramedics had to break the door down and rush her to the hospital. Worse, sometimes I feared I'd come home and she would be dead. That happened especially when I called home and she didn't answer. I really thought she might have died. That was a real possibility for a while in our odyssey with this illness so I wasn't just a stressed man who was imagining things.

I gathered myself and walked to the door of the bedroom and peaked inside. The room was cold. The light was dim. Medications covered the top of her nightstand. The tops were off of a couple of the prescription bottles. A few were upside down. One had fallen on the floor. A small and frail body huddled under the covers barely moving with each breath. The mask of pain and illness was etched on her face. Her hair was thin and disheveled. Her skin looked ashen. Her face was drawn. I didn't wake her. Her sleep was too hard to achieve. She was up most nights unable to sleep because of the pain and discomfort the symptoms caused. If she was lucky she'd finally get to sleep from sheer exhaustion and the aid of medications. I just gazed for a few moments and went back into the other room. Watching my wife suffer during those darkest days of this experience was the most emotionally painful thing I've ever endured.

She'd be up in a few hours and then I'd make dinner. We would talk some and then start our nightly rituals. For her that meant more medication and a long bath in oatmeal. Then she would have to put all kinds of ointments on her parched skin. For me it meant eating dinner, showering, and trying to sleep through the sounds of the television she'd left on for company and the faint sounds of sobbing coming from the bathroom. When I heard her crying I would get up and go to her. Sometimes I held her hand. Sometimes I just sat with her. It was like this every night for what seemed an eternity. I don't know how she made it through those days and I don't know how I did either.

Action Plan

1. Put things into perspective

Remember the body you're looking at isn't your spouse, it's just a sick body. The real person you love is the spirit on the inside. This realization can help you keep the right perspective when you see the ravages of the illness on their body.

2. Know your limitations

Make sure you do your best and when you have, accept that you have done your best. You're doing the best you can and give yourself credit for it. When you see a loved one suffering the first thought is "What can I do?" This is followed by "Am I doing enough?" Chances are you are doing all that you can. You have to accept that many chronic illnesses don't have a cure and all you can do sometimes is manage the pain and the symptoms. This doesn't mean you give up because it's possible the right treatment or combinations of approaches is out there and you just haven't found it. But don't beat yourself up thinking you aren't doing enough or should be doing more if you can't.

Questions to Consider

1. What is your gut feeling when you see your spouse suffering?
2. What are your coping methods to handle your spouse's suffering?
3. What can you do to comfort your spouse? What are your limitations?

Journal idea

What's the ugliest part of the physical suffering your spouse has to endure? What is the toll this takes on you and how do you cope with it?

"In Sickness and in Health"

I often wonder how many people really think about their marriage vows before they say them. The euphoria of love and romance often blinds us to the realities of the vows we are taking as we stand at the altar. One of those vows, "In sickness and in health," is little more than an abstraction to most of us as we are standing there in health with our whole lives and dreams in front of us. My wife had some complications with her health when we married so I did actually think about the "In sickness and in health" line more than most people might consider it. But I could never have imagined the effects of a major chronic illness. That's something that you just can't prepare for. The next section is an example of living the vows I have taken.

The Dilemma

One of my books, *The Hidden Lover,* had just been published and I was touring to promote it. People outside publishing look in and think a book tour is a glamorous trip flying around the country, being flocked by adoring fans, and spending time on the air with television and radio hosts. It is a rewarding experience but it is also one of the most grueling and challenging things I've ever done. I've been on five book tours and it never really gets easy. You fly into a city and you're whisked away to your hotel, where if you're lucky, you have time to sit down for a quick lunch before starting a long day of visits to television stations, radio stations, bookstores, and special events. That evening you get back to your hotel and basically collapse. You order room service and watch television. Then you go to bed early because at five o'clock the next morning, the driver will be there to take you to the airport, where you will blast off to another city and do the same thing over again there. Honestly, after about three cities you have to rehearse remembering which city you are in. And you don't care about the day of the week anymore.

As an author at the largest publisher in the country I had to generate sales to keep my books flowing. The tour wasn't a vacation for me. It was work and I put it as my highest priority. During a tour basically I have to be available 24/7 for calls, interviews, and sometimes to fly out to do a major show on short notice. While I'm on the ground or in the air my publicist is working overtime to secure these bookings for me and I have to be ready to go. In essence, the author is part of a team consisting of the publicist, author, and whomever is sponsoring the event.

My publicist lined up some good events for me on the tour and systematically, one-by-one, I'd completed them. Then we came to the last leg of the tour, which was a quick jaunt up to Dallas. Living in Austin that was an easy trip to make so I figured I'd fly up and back in the same day. The day I was supposed to catch my flight, Jamey had been having some painful swelling. It was a reaction to the medication she was taking, but both of us had been through this before and we didn't really think a lot of it. When I called from my office, however, she sounded worse. She could hardly talk because of the pain she was experiencing.

Flipping into dutiful husband mode, I immediately thought, "I can't fly out with her feeling this way." But we both knew that unless the situation was absolutely critical I needed to be on that plane. It was my business and I had to do it. Missing tour dates not only doesn't sell books, I would miss media that led to speaking events, and my publisher might see me as a risk when new projects were proposed. So it wasn't really as simple as just not going.

Making matters worse, it was a cold blustery day and the temperature was dropping. The wind was howling and the clouds were dark and gloomy. It all created an ominous backdrop for what was starting to be a boiling feeling in the pit of my stomach as I passed the University of Texas and got on Highway 35. Gritting my teeth, I clenched the steering wheel. "Why does everything have to be so complicated?" It's times like this that can be dangerous for the caretaking spouse. I slipped into a game of "what if," and that is a game that only sets one up for frustration. What if she wasn't ill? What would be different? I pictured myself in a different car—a luxury car instead of the little economy car I was in. I thought about how we wouldn't have lost our dream home. I imagined the children we would have had already. As a result, I just became more frustrated.

My cell phone rang. Jamey was on the other end. She was talking through the pain, trying to be brave. The boiling in the pit of my stomach grew worse. Now I felt a mixture of sympathy for her and anger at the situation. Even my chest was starting to hurt. It was too much pressure, too many decisions, all of which were critically important. As I looked at the weather, which was growing worse by the minute, I took it as a sign. This trip just wasn't meant to be.

I dialed my publicist on the cell phone. She was happy to hear from me because she'd just booked another television show and a newspaper interview for the Dallas trip. She excitedly talked about the details when I interrupted her abruptly. "Jill, I'm not going to be able to go to Dallas today." I was blunt and matter-of-fact. "Jamey is really ill and I need to stay home with her. There's nobody available to stay with her while I'm gone."

The phone was silent for a few moments. "William, I don't understand. I have lots of things lined up for you and I've worked really hard to make this a good leg of the tour." She was getting emotional. The first half of her statement was tinged with a little anger and the second half sounded like a schoolgirl pleading with a parent.

"There's nothing I can do about it. Believe me, if there were another way I would get on that plane or I could even drive up later tonight. But she's in bad shape. I can't leave her."

She made one more plea but the finality of my decision was in my grave tone of voice. She hung up with the words, "The bookstore is going to be really disappointed and I can't reschedule these media interviews."

It was a short conversation. I felt terrible. As if I'd let the team down. Then, it started to snow. It had been snowing intermittently for a couple of hours but now it was really starting to come down fast. It was actually snowing, a rare sight in Austin. All of the cars slowed down as snow swirled around us. The traffic quickly came to a standstill and we were all stuck on the freeway bumper-to-bumper. Nobody moved because we couldn't see anything in front of us.

I turned on the radio to get a news update. It was snowing hard all over Austin and the freeways were jammed. The weather was supposed to get worse. Schools were closing and people were trying to get home to safety. Then the power started going out in different parts of the city. From the freeway I didn't see any lights on at the gas stations, restaurants, and buildings. And the airport was closed too! As my usual 15 minute drive slowly turned into a 2 hour, inch-by-inch, crawl home, I felt vindicated.

I called my publicist back to tell her about the weather. I told her things worked out for the best because the airport was closed and I couldn't have flown, or even driven out, anyway. All the way up to Dallas, Texas was experiencing one of the worst winter storms in recent history. I told her we could now officially blame it on the weather.

In this case all ended well. But that's not always the way it goes. Every day the spouses of the chronically ill face the same, and even far more difficult decisions. Some of them have to travel. Some have to work long, exhausting hours. These decisions place a lot of stress on us and we have to recognize how this is affecting us and our relationships, because it does. None of us have superhuman emotions that can withstand the constant stress without reacting. It's how we react that we have to focus on.

To avoid the anger, some go into deep denial. They always put on a happy face and play the dutiful role even though they don't really feel it. Others wallow in it. They take on a sick-spouse role instead of being a caretaking spouse. They unofficially withdraw from the world. They continue to show up for work. They continue to parent. But inside they die a little each day. And with that their hopes, dreams, and excitement for life fade away until they are just a shell of a person. No longer living, just existing.

Last, some avoid it. They leave. I don't know the desertion rate for spouses of the chronically ill, but I've heard enough poignant stories of spouses who left because they couldn't take another day to know that the number has to be high. To be honest, I would like to stand up and scream from the highest mountain how terrible it is to divorce a chronically ill person. One part of me wants to condemn those people as cowards who deserted their duty, like a soldier who slips away in the night to avoid the big battle where all are needed to fight for the cause. But, we all have different stress thresholds and what is a breaking point for one person is just another day in the life of others. I can't sit and judge people and say bad things about them. How do I know that a much worse set of circumstances might not have developed had they stayed? It's not for me to say.

Action Plan

1. Don't play "what if."

That's one of those self-tormenting psychological games people play with themselves and can't win. Deal with the here and now. It's okay to dream about a time when things will be better. But that's very different from thinking about the way you feel things "should be." The situation is what it is. Believing things are supposed to be a certain way is a sure way to get your self angry, frustrated, and depressed. Be where you are right now and make the best of it.

2. Think about the consequences of your actions.

Don't be quick to jump and be a martyr. Sometimes the work you must do, places you have to go, or hours you have to put in, may take you away from your ill spouse but it may be what you need to do to support them in the long run. Being a martyr may seem heroic and make you feel you did the right thing, but it may actually be a foolish act born of emotions—an act that ultimately does more harm than good.

3. Find peace in your actions.

You will have to make some tough decisions in order to support your spouse. When you find yourself having to sacrifice, make sure to make peace with what you are needing to do. Acting out of mindless dutifulness isn't good because you don't feel it in your heart. Later, you might become bitter and resentful.

Questions to Consider

1. When was a time you had to sacrifice for your spouse? How did you feel about it?

2. What is your strategy for making sure you perform at work while also fulfilling your role as caretaking spouse?

3. What advice would you give other caretaking spouses on balancing the roles of working and caretaking?

Journal Idea

What was an occasion when chronic illness forced you to make a sacrifice for your marriage? How did you respond? Have you been able to make peace with these sacrifices? How?

Take Care of the Caregiver

When your spouse is ill you have a greater chance of developing a serious illness, or even of death. This phenomenon is called the "caregiver burden" or "caregiver bereavement." It's real and it is something we should all pause and seriously consider. This is exactly why I struggle with the term "well spouse." Things aren't "well" for the well spouse because this person is juggling multiple roles which create major stress.

Actually, in my opinion there's no such thing as a well spouse and an "ill spouse." I don't like these terms because they imply one spouse is sick, even burdensome, and one spouse is well, as though nonaffected. A couple is a psychological, emotional, and physical system. They are an integrated unit of mind, body, and soul. When one person is ill the system itself is ill and it is not going to function at maximum capacity

A joint study by Harvard and the University of Pennsylvania published in the *New England Journal of Medicine* in 2006 provides insight into this phenomenon. The results of the study suggest that the spouses of seriously ill patients are significantly more likely to develop life threatening illnesses themselves. This higher risk of death and serious illness is related to factors such as stress, emotional strain, lack of daily practical help, and financial challenges.[*]

I was shaken by the news that Dana Reeve, actor Christopher Reeve's widow, died of lung cancer at the young age of 44,[**] particularly because she was not a smoker. Although I don't know the details of her life and death, perhaps she is an example of the effects of stress on a caretaking spouse.

Does this mean all caretaking spouses are doomed? Are caretaking spouses all heading for illness themselves? The answer is no, because it all depends upon each caretaking spouse's approach to the situation. We need to take care of ourselves because we are at a higher risk for becoming ill too.

Here are some of the factors that combine to potentially affect the health and wellness of the caretaking spouse:

---

[*]   N.A. Christakis et al. and P.D. Allison, "Mortality After Hospitalization of a Spouse." *New England Journal of Medicine* 354, issue 7 (2000): 719-730.

[**]   John O' Neil, *New York Times*, March 7, 2006.

- Most of us have to work overtime, if not an extra job to make up for the lost income of our spouses and the additional costs of the illness. This extra work creates both physical and mental fatigue and often leads to emotional strain. You have to guard against anxiety and depression creeping in.

- You have a greater share of the domestic chores. Things that would ordinarily be split between two healthy spouses are usually handled only by the well spouse. For example, after working overtime or getting off from your second job, you also have to stop at the grocery store to do the shopping, come home and cook dinner, then mow the lawn.

- As the caretaking spouse you play the role of nurse, physical thera-pist, patient advocate, and counselor. Your responsibilities may include preparing special baths, rubbing on a salve, or a therapeutic massage. You also make calls to doctors, pharmacists, and clinics. You probably spend additional hours on the internet researching the condition and searching for new answers.

- If you have children or other dependants (including pets), your respon-sibilities are multiplied exponentially in even more categories.

I Found Relief in Food

With so many things weighing on them, it's no small wonder that many care-taking spouses don't seem to have the time to take care of themselves. I can totally relate to this. During the first five years of this experience I stacked on 30 pounds. I remember standing naked in front of a mirror inspecting every fat inch of my body. The happy and athletic-looking guy on the cover of my first book in 1998 was buried under 30 pounds of blubber.

The funny thing about getting fat is that you don't see it coming. It happens in small subtle ways. You can't wear a certain pair of pants. Or a favorite shirt gets tighter. Then you have to get new pants. You notice your profile in a win-dow as you approach the building you work in. Perhaps a friend or coworker makes a comment. And then, boom! Suddenly, it feels you've turned into this human helium balloon. You look at the scale and cry foul but it's true. You're fat! The question for you at that point is why? What am I doing that let me get to this point? What changes do I need to make to correct this?

Everyone has a way they deal with stress. Some people try to drown their troubles in alcohol. Others try to chase away the blues with crack, meth, or a cocktail of prescribed medications they collect like candy. Others seek solace through compulsive sexual acts. And some lash out in aggression. Those are just a few of the self-destructive coping mechanisms people find. The methods are as vast as the types of people on earth.

But for many Americans, eating is self-medication for managing stress. Eating provides pleasure both psychologically and physiologically. It's also socially acceptable and can be done right out in the open. If you like marijuana you can't just whip out a joint in your office. But you can sit in your office and inhale a big piece of chocolate cake. You can't sit at your kid's Little League game and light up a crack pipe. But you can have a chili dog with cheese, fries, and an extra large Coke and get a high from that. The psychological relief it provides is that you are getting pleasure. You're doing something for yourself and it is making you happy. Chemically the high fat and high sugar foods are also affecting your body in a way that gives you a high.* That's why overeating is the drug of choice for many people.

I'm no different. My drug of choice is desserts.

Looking back on it, I can see exactly how the 30 pounds piled on. I was working full-time as a professor and also teaching extra classes because we needed the money for health-care issues. In addition to that, during the early years of Jamey's illness I was in graduate school completing my doctorate. When I wasn't taking care of my wife's various needs, I was grading papers or deep in my studies. Meanwhile my parents were growing frail and needing my help too. In hindsight, I don't know how I didn't just melt down altogether. My whole life had become working or caretaking. That's when I started eating because it tasted good, which made me feel good. I was getting high on the food. If we had something tasty for dinner, I'd have a second portion without thinking about it. I started reaching for extra pieces of pie. I bought giant chocolate chip cookies. Cheese cakes, carrot cakes, lavishly iced white cakes, any cakes! I was eating more calories and fat in the dessert than in my entire meal. It was the perfect combination for weight gain: high stress, low activity, and high fat intake.

I'd still make time for a short walk or going to the gym but that was counteracted by the sweets I was eating. The weight stacked on and my pants didn't fit. I found myself buying new pants to fit my girth and the old regular-sized pants were being shoved further and further toward the back of the closet. I was changing sizes faster than I could explain or rationalize to myself. When I finally stepped on a scale I was horrified. It was a rude awakening. I felt as though someone had splashed cold water in my face.

At the same time, I also started having a health issue that concerned me. I was experiencing trouble breathing while asleep. I went to a doctor for a routine checkup still in denial about having gained that much weight. His scale

---

*   Diane Martindale, "Burgers on the Brain," _New Scientist_, February 1, 2003.

confirmed it with even a few more pounds than my home scale. He preached a sermon to me about the dangers of carrying excess weight. He also cautioned me about other conditions I might be at risk of developing if I didn't make a change. I took it to heart because I'd already had the same talk with myself.

I had committed the cardinal sin of caretaking: I was so concerned about everyone else and I was putting their needs so far ahead of mine that I wasn't taking care of myself. While it may appear noble it is not at all wise. If you run yourself into the ground, what good will you be to your spouse and family? If you don't take care of yourself, you can't take care of anyone else.

I knew I had to do something to turn this around. Fad diets were out of the question—they do more harm than good. I wanted a healthy plan that I could really live with. Basically, I had to change my habits. Since my Jamey had been a personal trainer before she became ill, I turned to her for help and she put together a sensible program for me. First she told me to write down everything I ate for two weeks. I did, and then we calculated my calories. I found a website that had calorie information for all types of food and used it to measure my caloric intake. Then we calculated the number of calories I needed to eat to be the weight I desired.

I started counting calories and dedicated myself to an exercise program featuring alternating days of 30-minute walks, swimming, and weight training. Soon people at work were noticing my weight loss. Next I pulled my old pants from the back of the closet where they had been banished when I started gaining all the weight. Suddenly sweaters and shirts I couldn't wear came back into my wardrobe. The inches and weight continued to drop. I also stopped having problems sleeping.

I want to emphasize that nothing else changed. Jamey didn't get any better. I didn't have a lighter load of courses to teach. I was still as busy as ever. However, *I* changed. And that's the only thing I really can control. Remember, if you don't take care of yourself, you can't care for anyone else. Right now, as I sit here writing this I'm dressed for the gym because after I write this line and save this to my hard, drive I'm going to work out.

Action Plan

1. Stay in shape!

As I said earlier, of course you don't have time. But you must make the time. Exercise; eat good, healthy foods; and make sure you get some daily quiet time. My quiet time is in the morning when Jamey is asleep. There's not a sound in the house and I look forward to that as a time to get my thoughts together. I often combine it with some light yoga stretching and then I eat breakfast in the silence.

2. You must have a life beyond the illness.

If you don't have a life beyond the illness, you are being unfair to your spouse as well as yourself. I know the idea of you being out playing softball or walking through an exhibit in the museum defies the saintly image of the doting caretaking spouse sitting bedside. But if you don't refresh your mind, soul, and body you'll ultimately wear out, and you may need a caretaker yourself.

For example, I found a life beyond the illness by going to graduate school. Stepping out of my unpredictable world and into the regimented and calculated academic world, provided relief for my mind. It was something that made sense because it moved along a finite track from start to finish, unlike the illness which was unpredictable and filled my life with variables and question marks. Instead of being stressful, graduate school was stress relieving because it forced me to think deeply about something other than the illness and what it had done to our lives. Today, I'm happy to say that I earned a master's and a Ph.D. in psychology during all of this.

Your job is to keep living: to earn income, to provide good conversation and warm hugs, and to bring a sense of normalcy and life into the household. Your spouse is depending upon you to do that. If you mirror the sorrow and pain they are experiencing they will only feel worse.

But watch out for a potential backlash. Sometimes the ill spouse feels guilty and ashamed and your achievements or busy living life can actually make them feel bad because they feel they are a drain on you or that you are going on without them. This is tricky. Let me warn you, however, the answer isn't to stop living your life and become a plaster saint by the bedside. The answer is to reassure them that they are in fact an integral part of your life and your achievements. You may need the help of a professional with this, depending upon the depth of the anger, pain, and resentment. The entire illness scenario does more than just trigger the physical pain. It also brings many raw emotions and unresolved issues to the surface for both of you involving things beyond your relationship that may go back as far as childhood. But don't let it fester. Address it.

3. Dump the stress

We all need to find constructive ways to dump stress, like trash, into a trash can. I have a number of things I like to do. As I said above, I enjoy exercising. I also play video games on my Xbox. I listen to music frequently. My wife and I watch a lot of comedies on DVD.

4. Have a spiritual grip

You're going to need more than just good intentions and exercise. Talking to God is very therapeutic for me. I'm not speaking of a God sitting on a throne with a fistful of lightning bolts. Nor some image in the clouds. I'm talking about a real and personal oneness with all creation that makes me feel safe and empowered.

I also have affirmations that I put in key places that will pop out at me. For example, I have a small card on my desk on which I've written "Expect a miracle today. Create miracles through action. Accept the miracles." I've had this on my desk for years. It reminds me to think of the possibilities of doing something to bring my thoughts and prayers into action, and to accept the fact that the answers to things I want and need may present themselves in ways I did not anticipate and above all, to trust God and go with the flow.

You may or may not be a Christian and I'm not writing this to proselytize, just stating my experience. But I can tell you that you will not make it in this journey of trials without a firm spiritual practice in your life. The chronic illness is bigger than you and your spouse and much of it takes place in a way that is beyond our reasoning and certainly beyond our physical capabilities.

Questions to Consider

1. What are some social activities you can have that will enhance your feeling of well being?
2. When was the last time you had a physical exam? Have you talked to your physician about ways to optimize your health?
3. What adjustments do you need to make to your daily schedule to make quiet time for yourself?

Journal Idea

What are you doing to take care of yourself physically, emotionally, and spiritually?

Let Somebody Help You

One of the biggest lessons I've learned during this experience is the value of accepting help. Since childhood, I've been a person who loves to reach out and help others. But being the helper most of the time led me to the mistaken belief that my only role was to provide help. But that isn't the case. In reality, one day you may be the one helping others and another day you may be the one needing help. In life, one has to learn to be gracious in giving as well as in receiving.

A good friend of mine, Episcopal Bishop Greg Rickel, has been a constant spiritual inspiration and support for us. He is one of the few men who could actually get a message into my stubborn head about accepting help. He gave me some words of wisdom on receiving help that I shall never forget. I told him that the church had helped us so much that I felt I owed them more than I could ever repay. I even felt ashamed. Then he said to me, "You've been helping others all your life, now it's time for you to let others help you. Other people need to help in order for them to grow. You have to let it happen." He was right. Those words resonated with me and changed my view of receiving help.

Earthly Angels

"Practice random acts of kindness" is more than a phrase on a bumper sticker. Many people actually live that way. I know because we have directly benefited from the love and compassion of people who have reached out and helped us. Just as there are cold and terrible people in the world, there are those who are warm and overflowing with the desire to be of service to others. These are truly altruistic souls who help not for financial gain or notoriety, but simply because they have love in their hearts. These people have done things for us that I can never fully thank them for. Sometimes these angels in the flesh are friends we've had for life and sometimes a stranger has been our hero. I've learned in this experience that there are lots of good people in the world. They come in all colors, sizes, classes, and education levels.

Here are just a few of the blessings we've received from earthly angels in our lives during this experience:

When we moved away from Houston I had to start my new job and we left our home with a lot of packing unfinished. Two of our best friends, went to the house with their kids and actually packed all of the remaining items and stored them at their house. They wouldn't accept one dime in payment.

Anonymous members of our church in Austin donated several costly series of acupuncture treatments for Jamey. To this day we don't know who these people were. Later, another anonymous donor blessed us with one thousand dollars of ultra violet blood irradiation treatments for Jamey.

Members of the church, both in Austin and in Houston, brought communion to our home every week when Jamey was too weak to get out of bed. They routinely took Jamey to medical appointments while I was at work. When Jamey had a rough time after one of her medical treatments in Austin and I had to lecture that evening at the university in Houston, another generous soul went to the hotel, collected Jamey's luggage, and then went to the clinic to get her. He proceeded to drive Jamey two-thirds of the way to Houston where another friend met them and drove her the rest of the way home!

A good friend of ours came by and regularly cleaned our apartment and would not accept any payment.

A holistic nurse practitioner gave Jamey discounted and free treatments.

A couple from church, with whom we became good friends, once spent the entire day with us at the hospital when Jamey had to go to the emergency room. They also became close confidants and a source of spiritual inspiration for us both.

My parents, and members of Jamey's family, provided us with financial assistance during some really critical times.

My brother-in-law acted as mission control while we evacuated Houston when hurricane Rita was threatening to blow the city off the map. I had a wife in precarious health and two frail parents in the car. Without his navigational help throughout the twenty-three hour ordeal from Houston to Dallas, we would have never found the quickest routes out of the congestion. He and Jamey's sister also graciously moved to one of the upstairs bedrooms in their home, so that we and my parents could stay in their master bedroom on the first floor.

A good friend and his girlfriend dropped everything in the middle of the day to help Jamey when I was out of the city and she was really in need.

A Stephen Minister from our present church home spends time with Jamey one-on-one each week. This wonderful woman has become more than just a visiting minister, she and Jamey have developed a special friendship that has given my wife a tremendous boost in morale.

There are so many people who have done so much for us that I could continue to go on with this list. Their involvement in our lives has always been at critical moments. These people have truly been the eyes, ears, arms, and legs of God.

Action Plan

1. Don't be proud

Pride is probably the most dangerous mentality to have when you are a couple facing illness. The bottom line is couples facing illness need a lot of help, support, and resources. A person full of pride will deprive him or herself as well as their spouse and family of the things that are available to them. That's unfair and only serves to make the situation worse.

2. Don't feel guilty about being helped

Surely one day you'll be helping the very people who are helping you. If not them, you'll be helping someone else in the same way by paying it forward. Helping is love in action.

3. Realize it's a blessing to be helped

It's not wise to refuse help when it is offered in love. In the situation couples facing illness deal with daily, the smallest things can make a big difference. Just someone helping you make a few calls, or dropping by the store for you, can allow you to get something else done, or even have some free time.

Questions to Consider

1. Have you asked your friends, relatives, or organizations (church, social, etc.) for help?
2. Do you believe the kindness you extend to others will return to you?
3. Why do you think it is hard for some people to accept help?

Journal Idea

How do you feel about accepting help from others? What are some ways in which others can help you?

What Works for Us

As I conclude, I want to leave you with a few things that we do to have a life beyond illness. Some of these are summarized points from earlier chapters and a few are mentioned here for the first time in the book. Couples facing illness have many things in common. However, each couple has circumstances that are unique to their situation. That's why I can't tell you exactly what to do in your situation, but I can tell you what has worked for us in ours in the hope that it will give you some insights.

1. Prayer, meditation, and visualization

I've found it very beneficial to take passages from the Bible and meditate upon them. As I've said before, I also imagine things the way I want them to be. What's important isn't whether they become those imaginings or not; it's the exercise of thinking that way that creates doorways to new great things happening.

2. Visualizing

This is critical for me. I'm a visual person so I need to see things. I visualize when I meditate. But Jamey and I also post photos and motivational sayings around the house. As I mentioned earlier, these reminders aren't just over the door. We have them in places where they will be noticed.

3. Don't blame God

I realize that illnesses happen as the result of being physical beings in the world in which we live. Part of having a body is the fact that it can become ill or injured. I don't think God is sitting back assigning illnesses to people. On the contrary, a loving God would want you to be healthy. But God isn't somewhere walking around with a cosmic goody bag full of treats and prizes that you get to redeem for different good deeds and pure thoughts.

4. Use Positive psychology

Focus on good things and positive thoughts because that plants the seeds that bring about more good. I can't emphasize this enough. If you dwell on things that make you feel bad, then you'll feel bad. If you think about things that are positive, you can consciously push yourself into a better direction. This certainly doesn't mean everything will go your way just because you're thinking positively. But it will help you handle your stress level much better and that is important to your overall health and personal performance.

5. Eat clean food

Eat clean foods that nourish your body and don't fill you with chemicals, pesticides and hormones. Buy organic fruits, vegetables, and milk. Eat meats that were raised in a free range environment and without steroids or hormones. Yes, it will cost more. But in the long run, what is your health worth to you?

6. Get exercise, rest, and laughter

Exercise is my number one stress reliever. Jamey has had great improvements in her health from exercise. You don't have to work out as if you're going to the Olympics. Even a simple walk every day can improve your health. If you can't exercise due to your condition, perhaps someone can help you at least get outside in the sunlight for a change of environment. Be sure to consult you physician for a health assessment before beginning an exercise program.

Do whatever is necessary for both partners to get adequate rest. This not only aids the body in healing but also helps the mind and one's perspective stay balanced and rational in the midst of stress. You may have to sleep during the day or take small naps after work or on the weekend, but whatever you do don't neglect your need to rest.

Laughter is truly one of the best medicines. It stirs up endorphins, relieves tension, and breaks up the sober aspects of battling illness. Jamey and I watch funny movies and shows and read or listen to amusing stories. We also find time to act really silly, doing zany dances and amusing impersonations. Jamey sometimes does a dance that looks like an old 1930s tap review and I start clapping along and waving my arms. Of course, she has to do this carefully since she's restricted by the illness. But that just makes it even more hilarious. It's completely absurd and wacky and always makes us laugh, no matter what. My specialty is a variety of voice impersonations. I create characters and give them voices and I also mimic the voices of people I see on television. We also joke about ourselves and our situation with one another and close friends. A sense of humor is a powerful tool for surviving and living beyond the illness.

7. Support system

You need a support system of people who really care about you and have your best interests at heart. Some people are fortunate enough to have large support systems. Others may only have only a few people, or even just one person. Try to identify people who can be there for you in a number of ways such as services you may need, mental, and spiritual support, or just plain good friendship and conversation. You can often find support through your religious organization or even socially oriented groups you are affiliated with.

8. Investigate proactive and innovative medical approaches

As I've mentioned before we use a health-care team. Our team goes beyond traditional medicine. We use an integrative-medicine approach with open-minded MDs, homeopathy, osteopaths, massage therapy, and acupuncture. This may or may not suit you and that's okay. This is our approach. Above all, you need to feel comfortable and confident in your treatment choices.

9. Goal setting

We set clear and realistic goals to aspire to but we don't freak out if we don't achieve them. The goals are an affirmation that you are still living life and that your life goes beyond illness. People who have goals have a purpose in life. A reason to exist.

10. Music

Playing music in the house helps set a healthy tone. Silence is a beautiful thing. But sometimes you need to have music playing to help lift your spirits. Leave music playing in strategic places so that when you walk into the room you are calmed or energized by it.

11. Control the input to your brain

Jamey and I don't watch sad movies and we don't watch too much grim news. Of course we don't hide our heads in the sand, but once we know what's going on, we move on. We have a list of sad or deeply emotional movies we haven't seen that everyone else seemed to enjoy. When we don't have so much of our own baggage we plan to rent them. But for now, we need to keep it light.

12. Helping others

Jamey started this practice and now I've picked it up. Every day we individually try to do something for someone else. It doesn't have to be something big but just something that allows you to pass along some positive energy. We also do charitable giving on our own small scale.

Being ill or in a relationship with an ill person often puts you on the receiving end of things. But when you turn it around and you are blessing others in your own way, you move beyond the psychological grip of the illness and that strengthens you. You're saying, "I'm viable and I'm not defeated by this illness because I'm making a difference in the world. I'm still here. I still matter."

PART TWO

Survival Handbook: When Chronic Illness Becomes Critical

Jamey Lacy July

Introduction

This section of the book comes from the heart of a book I began writing last year entitled, *Healing Outside The Bubble.* The truth is, I did not want to write this book because I never wanted to go through the throes of chronic illness and the physical losses and suffering that have been an ever-present part of this whole experience. Years of writing about wellness, fitness, nutrition, healthy body image, and health consumer topics still did not prepare me to write about this raw and painfully personal matter. Being an athlete and fitness professional for most of my adult life did little to equip me for the devastating crash into the brick wall of debilitating chronic illness. Even working with hundreds of clients in the special area of physical reconditioning and recovery from many types of illnesses and injuries failed to provide me with all that I needed to battle the uncharted areas of the baffling disease that assaulted my own body. In fact, after the "hit" as I looked upward from within the confines of my battered body, I immediately recognized that my professional knowledge of physical fitness and human health was really a double-edged sword. On one hand, it empowered me with sound knowledge about the human body, and especially a keen sense of my own physical health. However, on the other hand, knowing what I knew seemed to make the reality of my circumstances even more bitter to chew.

While all of us will experience the death of our physical selves at some point (and disease typically plays a large role in this), we are naturally inclined to believe that if the disease process happens to us, it will likely be later on in life as opposed to early on. When we are unexpectedly assaulted by chronic illness in these early phases of our lives, we are usually so unprepared that it turns our life upside down, along with the lives of those who are closest to us—our family and loved ones, business associates and partners. So when my husband and coauthor asked me to collaborate with him on his book, *A Husband, A Wife, and An Illness,* I recognized that the part of my book; *Survival Handbook,* which deals with surviving the critical moments of chronic illness would be the most beneficial tool for readers.

After all, being hit with chronic illness can be the ultimate test for anyone who is part of the human experience. I think it can be especially challenging for younger adults and those of us in the prime years of life, since most of us in this twenty-first century world expect to live the 80 to 90 years that is now considered a full lifespan.

While many people may experience a short-term setback from an illness or injury; the condition subsides after a few weeks or maybe months, so that their lives as they generally know them resume again. This may be one of the best things that could happen to any person because it gives one a truer understanding of what a gift our health is, along with our capacity or ability to carry out life plans and goals. This also enables us to resume living, and thriving, with a renewed sense of appreciation, determination, and inspiration.

But it is the long-term illness that lasts years and sometimes decades, that is the ultimate test of our bodies, minds, and spirits. It is also the ultimate test for those who love us—especially our spouses. It requires a true commitment that asks, "How deep do love and devotion go?" Chronic illness tests us in so many ways that those who are blessed with general health and ability may never know. It is like a great overbearing presence that ties up our ability to carry out the things we most feel called to in this life: loving and caring for our loved ones, utilizing our gifts and talents through work and hobbies, expressing our creativity and even our joy, and reaching out to others in our communities.

Because of the problems such as poor accessibility to medical insurance and health care provision, and the woefully inadequate knowledge of curing chronic diseases (as opposed to just treating or managing them), chronic illness can be much like a death sentence. It may be a lengthy journey, where many end up walking down the road of inevitable demise as their bodies succumb slowly but steadily to the progression of illness for lack of effective treatment and care. To make matters worse, most health professionals fail to address the spiritual aspects of our recovery. Although scientists and medical practitioners generally agree that our bodies, minds, and souls are all equally important parts of our being, most treatments address our physical health, paying little or no attention to our mental and spiritual healing.

So, how do we make sense of our lives once we hit that brick wall and are knocked off of our feet from the physical limitations and weakness, pain, and other hardships that accompany chronic illness? How do we cope mentally and spiritually with the wreckage of our physical bodies? After all, we are humans who, unlike our four-legged mammal counterparts, have the gift of free will or the ability to rationalize and make decisions about our lives and existence. However, when we are bombarded by chronic illness, it often seems that this privilege is taken from us; we quickly realize we are not in control and may not even have the options to make our own choices in regard to our physical bodies, our health, treatment, and recovery. This can easily leave us feeling utterly displaced. We now have to reevaluate our life purpose and try to make sense out of this odd experience that seems to relegate us to the most basic mode of merely *surviving* as opposed to *thriving*. Yet our human nature, our soul instinct, yearns to go beyond the merely surviving mode and live in a state where we are thriving: co-creating, actively loving and caring for others, accomplishing goals in our professional and personal lives. All this can seem like grains of sand slipping through our hands as we face chronic illness.

In writing about my experience—the one I didn't want to have, or write about, I have charted some of the more difficult issues I've encountered and the steps I've taken to plow through the rubble of this unexpected roadblock known as chronic illness. In doing so, it has empowered me to face the demons of disease and discover some of the better routes for my recovery and find moments of peace in this process. It is also my fervent hope and prayer that sharing my experience with others facing chronic illness (or those who are affected by a loved one who is ill) may inspire them to stay steadfastly focused on their steps toward the various healing possibilities. And most of all … to remain hopeful in surpassing the phases of survival and finding a way to live and thrive beyond the illness.

Surviving the Critical Moments

Every person who has ever experienced chronic illness, or a serious long-term injury, knows that there are critical "911 moments" when we are supremely challenged, whether from physical pain and a peak of symptoms, or mental and emotional fatigue and the despair that often comes with these moments. Sometimes, when things really get tough, we are faced with all these things at once. During such times it may seem that we are unable to get through it and survive that very experience. I often find myself comparing it to walking through the fire to get to a better place on the other side.

Another analogy or example of this is the familiar concept of Our Creator reshaping me, as an artist would shape clay, and then, in order to set my newly created image and make it complete and strong, I must experience the heat of the kiln. But the truth is that when we are at that critical place with illness and pain, these analogies can just sound like platitudes and do little to provide comfort during these intense moments. As I write this, I am in the seventh year of battling a rare disease that took almost five years to diagnose. In the interim, this condition was treated by a hospital internist with high doses of steroids, which only served to weaken my immune system, allowing the condition to progress. If this wasn't devastating enough, the steroids caused immeasurable damage to my health in other ways.

In less than a year, I went from having maintained a lean, physically fit body for over 23 years (and being featured regularly in health magazines and publications), to literally a semi-invalid. My once healthy, strong bones and optimal mobility were ravaged by steroid-induced osteoporosis, which resulted in multiple spontaneous fractures in my hips, back, and ribs. Where just a few months earlier I had been able to power walk, hike, climb, and ride a bike, I was now only able to move about by using a wheelchair, scooters, and a walker. As a fitness professional, I had practiced all the necessary steps for maintaining healthy blood pressure and optimal weight, only to see my body distorted by over 30 pounds of pitting edema (long-term swelling of bodily tissues), and my healthy low blood pressure suddenly become seriously high. I also began having heart problems such as arrhythmia and debilitating bouts of chest pain, which included at least one minor heart attack. If all this weren't enough, the prescribed steroid medication also induced cataracts that required surgery on both of my eyes. Ironically, these conditions resulted from medication that did nothing to help alleviate the actual initial illness I was battling. Because this condition went untreated, it progressed to a more serious status. In the process, two more chronic conditions developed that were secondary to the main disease I was fighting. Both these secondary conditions probably would not have occurred had I been treated correctly and in a timely manner for the initial illness. My life as I had known it for nearly 23 adult years had been obliterated!

When my initial condition was finally diagnosed, the disease had progressed to the point where conventional treatment proved ineffective. Since that time, I have had to look to alternative or nontraditional methods of treatment. My loved ones (including my husband, who is an author and psychologist and several friends who are physicians, nurses, and social workers) have spent many hours researching the disease. Over time, we have found some alternative health treatments that seem to be effective but since they are extremely expensive, up to this point I have only been able to do short-term segments or cycles of these treatments.

To have been blessed in my work as a wellness consultant with the gift of helping thousands of others to improve their physical condition and overcome obesity and other health challenges, seemed a great irony as I was suddenly incapable of even walking, let alone exercising. It has taken a measure of strength, perseverance, and faith that I did not know I had to get through the last few years, as my broken bones have slowly healed and I've been able to walk again without assistance or the use of a special chair or walker. This is a far cry from the fitness pro and nutritional coach, competitive athlete, interactive mom, wife, sister, daughter, granddaughter, friend, and mentor that I had been for most of my adult life. Although I still experience pain from the fractures, it is less pronounced. I do have to be extra cautious in moving about, and I take a special bone-building medication for the osteoporosis. With the addition of the blood pressure problems, some eyesight issues, and carrying about 30 pounds of extra weight from the still-present edema, along with another 10 pounds gained from being unable to walk or exercise consistently while my fractures were healing, we are basically back to the place I was over five years ago. I say "we" because my husband (who is my main care provider) and my closest family and friends have also been drafted into this odyssey by virtue of loving me and being genuinely concerned about doing all they can to help me to recover.

I am still facing a nontraditional illness and secondary conditions that often leave me besieged with pain and an odd array of symptoms that create unimaginable bouts of respiratory challenges, internal and external swelling, and other unusual symptoms. Some of these include skin rashes, lesions, and unidentified splinter looking matter that comes out through my skin from head-to-toe, which incites acute allergic reactions.

Lowered immune function from both the medication and the initial condition makes it necessary for me to apply special protective ointments to my skin before going anywhere outside of our home—which is about a two hour process. To avoid extreme allergic reactions that typically result in systemic problems, I have had to avoid certain public places such as theaters and most auditoriums, pet stores, used book stores, copy stores, and restaurants with carpeting, and homes that have a lot of carpeting, draperies and pets. Although two of the many medical specialists I've seen have suggested that I would fare better by "living in a bubble," my husband and I are focusing on my potential for healing and recreating a healthy immune system—outside the bubble.

Because the chronic illness I am battling is relatively new on the empirical charts of medicine, we have had to face these conditions with very little support from the medical community. We have also had to navigate without the vitally important knowledge or road map that is available to others with more traditional diseases, which provides specific plans for treatments and cures along with validation, emotional support, and *hope*.

For those in similar situations to mine, who are facing chronic diseases that are not supported by viable treatment protocols, we are left with the ultimate truth: all healing comes from Our Divine Loving Creator and the doctors, medical treatments, and other remedies are merely vessels for that Divine Healing and renewal. However, for even the most faithful, the absence of healing methods or specific steps toward recovery can challenge our sense of progress with our healing. This proves most difficult when we hit those critical phases where our condition worsens suddenly and symptoms are at a peak.

When we find ourselves in those critical moments, and I use the word "moments" tentatively, as moments may turn into hours or even days or weeks in some cases—we have to have a plan of action … something tangible we can do, think, and even say, to help see us through to the other side of the fire. We need a plan to help us endure the heat of the kiln until we are solidly set again.

Our chances for survival, healing, and renewal depend heavily upon how we respond mentally, emotionally and spiritually to withstand and overcome the most difficult periods of chronic illness. I think one of the greatest oversights by mainstream medicine is the fact that this industry fails to educate and train doctors and other health practitioners to help patients heal from perspectives other than just the physical. After all, we are not merely a physical body or human shell. We have physical, mental, emotional, and spiritual components that make up our unique and complex being. Therefore, if only one aspect of our being (the body) is attended to, the other areas of our being have less chance of experiencing the benefits of healing and renewal. Even more importantly, if the physical treatment or cure is lacking, or worse, un-established—then our only way to move forward is to address the nonphysical aspects of our healing which, in turn, always play an important role in helping our bodies to heal.

Even if our physicians and professional health practitioners overlook these vital facets of treatment, we can take steps to heal in these areas ourselves. This is especially important when we find ourselves in the midst of a crisis with chronic illness or disease. The following are some essential steps, in the form of a survival handbook that have helped me, and countless others we network with, to survive those critical moments.

† Avoid panic and fear, as they only serve to intensify pain and symptoms.

This step is the by far the most crucial, and perhaps the most difficult, in surviving critical health moments.

1) First, assess and identify, as calmly as possible, your situation: "I'm having a flare-up of my symptoms" or, "I've entered a critical phase with my condition either physically or mentally or both." As you recognize this, remind yourself not to panic.

2) Next, determine if you are in distress to the point where you need assistance. If you are having difficulty breathing, or your pains—especially if in your chest or head—are preventing you from speaking or breathing regularly, or you are experiencing numbness or signs of seizure, then you should summon immediate help. Have a phone near you at all times. If someone is typically with you in your home, keep a bell or whistle next to you. If you have had regular or even occasional episodes of this nature, you need to have an emergency assistance device. <u>Do not hesitate to summon assistance when you feel you are in serious distress.</u> An alarming number of people, especially women, have unnecessarily lost their lives simply because they didn't want to "bother" their physicians and loved ones. I will always remember the story of my dear friend's mother who died of a heart attack because she didn't want to inconvenience her family when she started having chest pains!

Whether you determine that you need medical assistance or feel you can survive this critical episode without professional aid, you'll be more likely to get through this phase more successfully if you can take specific steps to help alleviate fear and tension.

3) Try to take at least 3 to 7 deep breaths. Twelve or more is even better. Relax as much of your body as you can and breathe deeply and slowly into your abdomen (diaphragm) letting your abdomen and chest rise as you inhale. Then, hold the air for 3 to 4 seconds and begin to let it out slowly through your mouth, placing your tongue lightly at the roof of your mouth so the air flows out around the tongue. As you inhale, envision healing oxygen going into the places that need it most; as you exhale, think of the pain or problem leaving your body along with the exiting air.

4) As you breathe, focus on relaxing every muscle from your toes to your head, including your face (brows, jaw, mouth,) and neck. Imagine every muscle softening and any pain melting away.

5) As you let your muscles relax, recall how you have gotten through other critical moments. Then, focus on one of your better moments— a period when you were symptom free, or close to it, and experienced a productive, positive day. Freeze-frame that image in your mind and remind yourself that this critical moment too, shall pass.

Here are some additional steps to help you get through the critical moments of chronic illness:

† **Pray to Our Loving Creator and ask for Divine Guidance.** Pray for clarity of mind and protection in this moment. Gently push away thoughts of panic, despair, and confusion. Quiet your mind to allow Divine Direction to become clear so you understand what you, or someone near you, can do at this time to assist in your recovery. Give thanks that God is supplying all your needs according to the Divine Plan. Remind yourself that God is the ultimate sacred parent; the perfect Father—Mother Creator who loves us more than we love our own children, mate, friends, and others (Matthew 7:11). Envision that love flowing through every single cell and rejuvenating and replenishing all cells, all organs, all tissues and health systems in your body. If you are able to speak without exertion or added discomfort, pray out loud and/or speak affirming scriptures or thoughts.

† **Medicine Checklist.** <u>If you are taking medication, make certain that you are following the instructions.</u> If there is something you can take, whether prescription or alternative remedies that can relieve your symptoms, do so at the onset of your flare-up or episode. **Note:** If you are experiencing severe pain, do not hesitate to take pain-relief medication that has been

prescribed by your doctor, or over-the-counter medications that he or she has suggested. There have been times when I have found myself thinking, "I can tough this out," but I have since discovered that long-term pain can cause undue stress on overall health as well as interrupt the body's natural production of endorphins, serotonin, melatonin, and other necessary chemicals. So when the going gets really rough, take your pain meds!

† **Hydrate.** Make sure you are drinking enough liquids (clear or caffeine-free drinks such as purified water, herbal teas, low-sugar 100% fruit juices, and eating fresh fruits and vegetables daily also helps hydration). Individuals with chronic illness cite dehydration as one of the more common conditions they are treated for when they have to go to the emergency room. Dehydration can exacerbate any health condition and impede natural body functions. The rule for consuming fluids is to divide your weight by two and that amount is the number of ounces of hydrating liquids you should consume each day. Do not count caffeinated coffee, teas, sodas, or alcoholic drinks because these will actually contribute to dehydration. For instance, if you weigh 140 pounds, you should be consuming half of that, which equals 70 ounces of fluids. Add another 8 to 10 ounces if you are exercising and/or using the sauna. If you are taking medications that dehydrate, such as some pain meds and antihistamines, allow for extra water and other healthy liquids to compensate. Be sure to drink fluids in increments of 8 to 25 ounces spread out every 1 to 3 hours throughout the day. For example, if you are drinking 8 ounces at a time, then you'll need to have at least one portion every one to two hours to equal approximately 70 ounces throughout the day and evening. Do not drink more than 32 ounces of water at a time because you can actually experience adverse health effects if you are consuming high amounts of liquids all at once.

† **Compassion Companion.** If you have a loved one or care provider nearby, call for them and just ask them to hold your hand or sit near you. Ask them to pray, speak affirmations and/or sing with you. Your care provider can also breathe deeply with you. I was once experiencing a bout with severe chest pains when one of my friends was present. The pain was preventing me from talking so we just quietly breathed together and silently prayed and visualized my chest being enveloped by the Healing Love of God. On some previous occasions when I had experienced this condition, she accompanied me to the ER. On other occasions, the symptoms actually subsided as I relaxed, breathed deeply, and prayed for and visualized healing. Had my symptoms worsened to where my breathing was too restricted or the discomfort became unmanageable, my friend would have called 911,

but that time they subsided after about 20 minutes. **Note:** <u>If you are having chest pains that are affecting your breathing or ability to move or speak and you are unfamiliar with this type of episode, it is best to call for medical emergency assistance.</u>

† **Cry.** Sometimes, if the pain or discomfort is too great, crying can actually provide a release. Don't feel bad about crying when you need to—even Jesus wept (John 11:35). Sometimes crying seems to require too much energy. In these moments, moaning can also be a healthy form of release. Sometimes when I'm experiencing a great deal of pain and anguish, I shut my door and cry or moan into my pillow to feel less inhibited about expressing my pain or despair. There have been some instances when screaming into my pillow, or punching the bed or pillow, has helped to release anguish and frustration over my health condition and thereby, also stress. Don't feel bad if you need to cry when it can help your body relax and overcome the episode more effectively. It is also a natural (God-given) mechanism for cleansing and purging grief and tension. Tears can wash us emotionally and mentally.

† **Forget about criticisms regarding "pity parties."** Most people I know who are going through critical phases of chronic illness and constant or frequent pain rarely have the luxury to have pity parties and actually have more trouble remembering to have self-compassion. We can be overcome at times by thoughts that we are a burden because of the illness we face, and more than likely have to fight off feelings of guilt or self-loathing. So instead of self-pity or self-loathing, allow yourself the same love and patience that you would a loved one. Think of it like this, if your child, beloved mate, or even a parent, sibling, or close friend, were in dire pain and suffering, wouldn't you feel compassion for them? In the same way, you may feel loathing toward the illness but you must learn to love yourself in the midst of this condition. Remind yourself each day that YOU are NOT the symptoms or physical effects of illness, YOU are beautiful and perfectly created and Divine Love lives within you through ALL that you experience. The illness can be painfully present and it can be shed, but your love and light-filled Spirit within will always be!

Over seven years of battling a devastating disease and all of its effects, I have slowly learned to view myself and the health challenges I'm confronting as separate entities. I have struggled over the years to overcome negative feelings about myself, especially the tendency to feel despair at how disease has ravaged my body and altered my physical appearance. I have even avoided mirrors and when I do see an image of myself, there are still times when I go through the gamut of feelings from shock at how unrecognizable I've become to feelings of sadness and hopelessness. As a teen and throughout most of my adult life, I've always had the self-discipline to exercise, eat healthy, and maintain optimal weight and physical shape. Even through the initial years of this illness I was able to push through the symptoms to maintain my weight and condition. Then, when bad medicine in the form of mega doses of prednisone incited a whole plethora of assaults to my body, leaving it truly battered, swollen, and literally broken, I had to reach deeply into the God Place within me. With the strength of the Love of The Holy Spirit I am beginning to see that I am still a lovely person and soul regardless of what the effects of illness have done to my physical image and being. This knowledge of who I truly am, from within, helps me to face the physical consequences of the disease I am overcoming and to replace despair and disgust with love and compassion for my innermost and truest self.

† **Massage.** If you are tense or hurting, sometimes just having someone massage your neck or feet, or the areas that are painful, can be helpful in relaxing the body and mind. If you are alone and are able, use a small handheld massager (Homedics makes a number of easy-to-handle units). Massage helps to increase blood circulation, which actually helps tissues to heal and eases pain and tension. This is also very helpful in calming the mind and body, leaving more capacity for the body to recover. If you shop around by phone or via the Internet, you can find some very good licensed massage therapists who are knowledgeable about treating individuals with chronic conditions. Some of these therapists can come to your home and may offer their services at a discounted rate when you purchase a series of sessions. Some insurance providers will also cover these services when prescribed by a doctor for pain management and/or to promote mobility. When I am receiving regular massage therapy in the form of deep tissue work, not only do I have more mobility but also less pain, which enables me to take less pain medication. For those of us forging through the battlefields of chronic illness, massage is not a luxury but a necessity. Massage therapy schools are also a good place to find therapists who are just completing their courses and therefore trying to build up their clientele. Interns at most schools will work for tips or a special cut-rate fee to get their practicum hours in.

† **Gentle Movement and Exercise.** Just like massage, gentle movement can promote circulation as well as relieve pain from physical and mental tension. Incorporate various gentle stretches along with deep breathing. If you are strong enough to stand or sit on the floor, gently stretch and reach from

side to side, lift your arm over your head and stretch one side of your body, then alternate. Start with 3 stretches on each side and do up to 12 if you can. If you cannot get up, you can do some of these simple stretches in bed. For instance, sitting up with several pillows supporting your back, and legs straight out in a V position, gently lean forward by pivoting at your hips (do not bend or bow your lower back) as you reach toward one knee to feel a gentle stretch in your hamstrings (the back of your legs) and inner thighs. Exhale (letting all of the air out) as you stretch forward then, inhale deeply as you return to an upright position. Repeat stretch toward the other knee. You can also lie on your back with a small towel or pillow under your neck, lower back, and knees, and bend one knee up and in toward abdomen while exhaling slowly. You may use your hands to gently help guide your leg. If you are able to, gently unfold your leg so that it is extended upward toward the ceiling. Bend your knee and bring your leg back in toward your abdomen/torso, then, slowly release it back onto the bed. Do the same with the other leg. These are just a few of the many different healing stretches that can be done when you are confined to bed or to your home.

➤ Remember, gentle movement and deep breathing can help to alleviate physical pain and tension. You can start with something as simple as walking around your home.

➤ If you are able to, try to do more specific non-impact exercises for just 8 to 12 minutes, in addition to increased circulation and oxygen intake, these additional exercises can strengthen muscles and boost your immune system.

The following are just a few samples of possible exercises to try if you feel strong enough: **Always consult your physician before beginning an exercise program.**

➤ **Pelvic Tilts**—Lie on your back (either on a firm bed or on the floor on an exercise mat) with a small pillow or rolled towel supporting your neck and head. Bend your knees and rest your feet flat on floor mat (or bed) and let your arms rest at your sides. Begin by breathing in while letting your abdomen expand outward with your pelvis slightly tilting forward—so that your lower back lifts slightly away from floor mat (while your buttocks remain on the floor mat or bed). Imagine as you are breathing inward that your middle and lower abdomen is a balloon and the air is expanding these areas. Then, as you exhale, imagine the air exiting those areas (so that the "balloon" or your abdomen flattens or deflates). As you exhale, your pelvic should tilt back into place resting firmly against the mat while your abdomen is flexing\into the lower back. Repeat 7 to 12 times. If possible, do this exercise once in the morning, once in the afternoon, and again in the evening.

> **Half wall squat**—Lean your shoulders and upper body and hips against the wall and slide your body down to lower into a half-squatting position by flexing your buttocks and bending your knees until the tops of your thighs are almost parallel with the floor. Raise upward returning to your original position by squeezing (flexing) your buttocks,/hips, and the tops of your thighs.

> **Step-ups**—At the foot of carpeted or wooden stairs, step up onto the first stair by placing your heel firmly on it while flexing your buttock and upper thigh. Then bring your other foot up onto the step. Lower off of stair and back down into original position with leading leg by placing your toes down first and then rolling back to your heel. As you are stepping back down, flex the opposite hip and/buttock to help lower your body without impact, to bring that leg back to the starting point at the bottom of the stairs. Then lower other leg down from stair so both feet are in starting position. Repeat 7 to 12 times and gradually work up to 18.

> **Water (non-impact) walking and squats**—If you have access to a pool, stand in the shallow end (with water level at waist) and walk 7 to 12 steps forward then turn around and walk back. Next, while standing with feet placed firmly on bottom of pool and your hands resting at the side of the pool, set your heels apart (about 2½ times the width of your shoulders) and your toes turned slightly outward, lower yourself into a half-squatting position. As you lower, bend your knees in the same direction of your toes, push outward with buttocks and hips and flex your inner thighs. Raise up into original (starting) position and repeat 7 to 12 times.

➢ **Upper arm stretch and tone**—While seated upright either in bed with 3 to 5 pillows supporting your back and keeping some distance from your headboard, or in a comfortable chair that supports your lower back, hold a 1 pound dumbbell in each hand OR a 3 pound dumbbell with a hand gripping each end of the weight. Sitting upright with your/ back straight and shoulders squared back, bring the weight(s) up over head until your arms are extended straight up toward the ceiling. Keep your elbows close to each side of your head as you lower the weight(s) with deliberate control by bending your arms (pivoting at the elbows) until your forearms, hands, and weight(s) are behind your head and parallel to the floor or bed. Then raise your arms and weight(s) back up into the extended position again. Start with 3 to 5 repetitions and work up to 12 to 14 reps for each arm.

If possible, have your care-provider or the backup support of a friend or family member the first time you begin to exercise. Your physician may prescribe exercise as reconditioning physical therapy to help ease pain, increase circulation and mobility, and prevent muscles from atrophying. If so, and you have health insurance coverage, there is a good chance that some of these sessions will be covered. You can also find certified exercise specialists and/or physical therapists who will come to your home. More information on healing exercises and stretches will be available in my upcoming book, *Healing Outside the Bubble.*

† **New Surroundings for Self Renewal.** Sometimes just moving to new surroundings such as another room can help you to feel better and find a calming place. If you have to rest, don't stay confined to your bed. Move to a sofa or comfortable chair in another area of your home. If possible, sit near a window and soak in the sunlight and scenery outside.

> If you are strong enough to walk and can step outside (and have an outdoor area that is safe and somewhat private), go out and look up at the sky, soak in the sunshine, or gaze at the stars. Feel your connection to the universe and think of how perfectly orchestrated the world is and how you too are part of that.

† **A hot bath with healing minerals or salts.** Soaking in the tub with special salts and/or minerals can be helpful in easing both pain and tension. If you have a loved one nearby or a care provider, ask them to prepare the bath and help you in and out.

† **The Amazing Power of Thoughts and Words.** Words and thoughts have proven to be one of the most significant factors in healing and recovery for me. This seemingly simple but amazing action of thinking positive thoughts and speaking affirming words out loud is not some hocus-pocus or gimmick. It is something quite powerful and real and too often overlooked. Both science and many spiritual disciplines point to this Universal Truth: what you think becomes you (Proverbs 23:7 "As one thinketh within oneself so shall one be"). Recently, interest in these principles has surged because of a book that claims that the secrets of success in life come from our thinking and saying that which we desire. But the truth is that these

principles have been effective through out time. If we think about or dwell on the negative, we feel negative energy, which impedes our strength and healing capacity. If we discipline our minds to focus on positive thoughts and images, our bodies also react positively and become more energized. It requires effort and focus, but when I am at my worst with physical pain and symptoms and I begin to direct my mind to think about healing images, it greatly improves my overall condition. If I speak these thoughts of over-coming and healing out loud, I almost always experience a reduction of physical symptoms and mental anxiety.

These are just a few of the many prayers and affirmations that have helped me;

Affirming Prayers

- ➢ God, You did not give me a Spirit of fear but one of Power, Love and a Sound Mind.

- ➢ Thank You, Beloved Jesus that I can, and therefore, I AM, doing all things through You, for You strengthen and sustain me.

- ➢ Thank You, Sweet Holy Parent, that you are supplying all my needs according to your riches in glory through Jesus Christ.

- ➢ Your Peace, Dear God, that passes all understanding, is keeping my heart, my mind, and my body through Christ.

- ➢ I am of God and have world-overcoming faith residing within me.

- ➢ No weapon (adverse condition) formed against me shall prosper, for my righteousness (my heart and intentions) are with You, Dear God.

- ➢ I thank You Beloved Creator, that You are on my side, that You are with me now; therefore, no person, thing, or circumstance (including any adverse condition or disease) can be against me.

Affirming Statements:

- ➢ I am strong, I am a Survivor, I have overcome so much more than this experience … this too, shall pass.

- ➢ My presence here is vital and therefore I am healing and transcending this pain (illness, injury, etc.)

- ➢ God's Divine Love and Healing Light are shining upon every cell in my body—perfecting all that concerns me.

➢ An abundance of Good is present in every area of my life, of which I am sharing and receiving.

➢ Through the Almighty Divine Power of Love within me, I rebuke and release all disease, disorder, and adverse matter from my body, soul, and mind.

➢ It is my Destiny and Divine Birthright to heal and to be blessed; therefore I am.

➢ The flow of good health is coursing through my body right now, illuminating every cell, and I am becoming stronger with each breath.

If you are unable to speak, say your prayers and/or affirmations silently. Listen to a tape or compact disc that offers relaxing music and healing prayers and/or affirmations. I recently created my own CD where I am speaking my favorite healing prayers and affirmations with calming background music. As in the above list I infuse my name or the word "I" into these prayers and affirmations so that the words become proactive. I do the same when I am praying and visualizing for others by incorporating their names into specific statements. I can't emphasize enough how powerful and miraculous this process can be!

➢ **Sing**. Even if softly, sing or hum one of your favorite songs, preferably one that is uplifting and inspiring. Research shows that your cells actually respond positively to the music you make.

➢ **Music.** If you have some relaxing tapes or CDs, ask your loved one or care provider to put one on. Most portable music players now have small remotes. Have a relaxing CD at the ready so that if you are alone and going through a critical moment, you can just press a button to start the music.

➢ **Laugh/Smile.** Think of something funny. Go over a funny episode in your life, a good joke, a movie, or show that made you laugh. If you have a care provider or loved one with you, ask them to share something funny with you,

➢ **Talk and Share with your Loved One:** If your loved one or care provider is not present, and you are physically able, phone a friend or someone who can talk with you and/or pray with you. Put the phone on speaker so you don't have to hold it. Talking with someone you trust and care about can really ease your tension and anxiety in critical moments. I like to think of these people as Human Lighthouses whom God puts into our path to help light our way.

The Emergency Room Dilemma

Emergency Room Nightmares

Most of us who have been through a long bout with illness, especially chronic disease, have invariably experienced the frustration of a hospital emergency room. It's difficult enough to find a medical practitioner who is willing to approach chronic illness with the objective of co-facilitating healing as opposed to blanketing the problem with medications, so it's not a great surprise that most ER physicians and medical professionals have even less insight into how to treat chronic diseases that have taken a critical turn. Adding to this problem is the fact that many chronic illnesses are categorized as atypical diseases (conditions that have not yet garnered a sizeable history of research). This often results in the medical care provider being unfamiliar with your condition, and, in the process, feeling incompetent, and frustrated for not knowing how to help. In an emergency environment this lack of knowledge can be potentially dangerous and even life-threatening to the patient. Doctors who were interviewed for a feature article In *Time* magazine, said that the thing that scared them the most was being a patient. They had even more qualms about being a patient in a hospital environment. The article also cites a 2003 Rand Corporation study, which found that only about half of patients received the necessary and appropriate attention and care for their conditions.[*] So when a patient enters the ER in a critical state with an illness that is complex and not generally understood by the medical community, she or he faces a greater risk of inadequate treatment combined with skepticism, a lack of compassion and tolerance, and, sometimes, out-and-out disdain.

As I mentioned at the beginning of this survival handbook, about three ½ years ago I went into the ER at a hospital in Houston when my symptoms from an undiagnosed chronic condition became critical, resulting in sudden overall swelling (I gained 18 pounds from edema in a 24-hour period) and respiratory problems. When I was admitted, the internist assigned to my case ordered that I be given mega doses of steroids intravenously. My weight prior to the sudden

---

[*]   N. Gibbs and A. Bower, "What Insiders Know About Our Health-care System That The Rest of Us Need To Learn," *Time*, pg. 43, Vol. 167, No. 18, May 2006

swelling was about 105 pounds, and the amount of steroids that I was given was 100 mg. That's almost 1 mg. of steroids per pound of body weight and approximately 40 mg. more than the manufacturer of this drug recommends for initial dosing in emergency situations. I remember pleading with the physician not to give me such large doses of this potentially dangerous medication, but he implied that he would have me discharged if I "refused treatment." I tried in vain to assure him I was not refusing treatment but felt that such high doses of steroids would be detrimental rather than beneficial to my health. Actually, half the dosage he recommended would very likely have been enough to treat the symptoms adequately.

As the week progressed, after much pleading on my part, this physician did finally reduce the dosage in half. However, anyone who has ever taken steroids for medical treatment knows that 50 mg is still a very high dose. What resulted in the following weeks as I tried to reduce the steroids and eventually wean my body off this drug, were recurring flare-ups that put me back in the ER several times. There, doctors would prescribe more of the steroids. Eventually, my adrenal glands and endocrine (hormonal production) system just went into sleep mode and I have as of this writing, been unsuccessful in getting off the prednisone. To make matters worse, when my condition was finally diagnosed, we discovered that steroids had suppressed my immune system, allowing the disease to progress more readily.

So that trip to the ER and the ill-chosen treatment by the dictatorial doctor ended up creating a living nightmare for me and my husband and our family. We are still searching for a cure for the chronic disease that I initially had, and fighting an unimaginable battle as we continue to search for ways to wean my body off the steroids and rehabilitate from their devastating effects. It's no wonder that when my condition becomes critical, we have to really deliberate on whether or not the ER is a viable option! I will add that while many of our trips to the ER have seemed frustrating and futile in helping me through critical flare-ups of my symptoms, there were some instances when the trip proved beneficial. One such time was when I woke with severe chest pains that made it difficult for me to breath. My husband called 911 and they sent an ambulance whereupon the emergency medical technicians were able to assist me with breathing, while also getting us quickly to the hospital where I was immediately seen by an ER physician.

The bottom line is that each patient, together with their loved ones and confidants, must assess whether the ER is going to be a place where they will receive some relief from the crisis they are going through; or be a crapshoot with little or no help, a long uncomfortable wait that may further aggravate your health condition, and a hefty bill.

Things You Can Do To Make The Most of the ER

One way to avoid the crapshoot experience is to call the hospitals in your area and speak with the managing physician or the director. Do this during the day-time hours in the middle of the week when the emergency care units are less busy, and when you are not in a critical phase. Find out who you or your spouse or care-provider should consult with about your condition to determine in advance what the ER can do for you during a health crisis. If you find a hospital with an ER that seems equipped to provide you with adequate care, keep the address and phone number nearby (next to your bedside and also in your wallet or purse). Also make sure your spouse or care-giver has this information.

The following are some additional things you can do to better prepare yourself for a trip to the ER:

- Have a small bag packed with a few days' worth of your medications and essential items, such as prescription ointments, daily supplements, personal toiletries, toothbrush, journal, Bible or spiritual readings, favorite book, etc.

- If you have health insurance, keep your insurance card at the ready. You can also have a typed list of everything on your card, e.g., the name, the address, and phone number of your insurance company, an emergency care contact number, and the I.D. number on your card, to keep in your pre-packed hospital bag. Make sure your spouse or care-provider has a copy. Have a typed list of all your medications, including the dosage and directions, in order of importance, along with a list of any medications or treatments you are allergic to. You may also want to have a concise list of your diagnosed conditions and symptoms, and a brief medical history. Also list your treating doctors and their phone numbers. Your spouse or care-provider should also have these lists and you should keep an extra copy with you in your wallet or purse at all times.

- Provide the ER physician with this information and inform her or him about your urgent symptoms or problems as concisely as possible. Remember, this is the emergency room and the medical staff has to work quickly.

- Have your spouse, or a family member or friend, accompany you to the ER. This person should be someone you trust who is familiar with your condition and situation. He or she should be prepared to help fill out forms, answer questions, and advocate for your care if necessary.

- If you and your spouse or care-giver are not satisfied with the care you are receiving once you are seen by the ER physician, you can ask to see the hospital director. The hospital may also have a patient advocate available to work with you in getting the care you need. Had we known this bit of information during my initial stay at the hospital where I was given mega doses of prednisone, we would have been more confident and persistent in requesting lower doses of this medication at the onset of my treatment.

- If you have a primary care physician such as an internist or infectious disease doctor, you can ask that the hospital contact her or him. You may ask that your doctor be informed of your condition and treatment while you are in the ER.

- Keep in mind that you can refuse any medication or treatment protocol if you have reason to believe it is unsafe or inappropriate for you. Note: If you do not have health insurance but are experiencing an emergency situation with your health, in many instances, the ER is obligated to admit you and treat you until you are stable enough to move to another hospital or go home.

Slaying the Mental Despair Monster

Sometimes our physical pain or discomfort from disease can be compounded by the mental anguish we feel from our circumstances. This is perhaps the toughest trial through the whole experience of illness. Although most people don't go into an illness depressed—feelings of depression, despair, hopelessness, and so on, can easily set in when chronic illness turns critical or difficult health conditions are endured for long periods. Also, various medications can alter your body chemistry and therefore create mood swings. Mental despair can sometimes seem overwhelming in the face of everything.

1) **Identify and consciously recognize your mental pain.** When we are hurting, it's easy to just slip into a state of autopilot with our anguish to the point where we are out of touch with our own feelings. When our eyes are opened to our experience, it allows us to move forward in seeking solutions and communicating effectively with those who can offer assistance. Some days I wake up feeling as though a wet, heavy blanket is on top of me. Immediately, I try to step outside myself or my feelings and look objectively at the problem or whatever may be behind this uneasiness. It may be that I've not had enough rest, which is vital to surviving chronic illness and pain. It may be that I've had a number of high pain days and/or some other difficulties in recent days, which seem to make everything harder to handle. When I am able to rationally assess the source of this higher level of mental anguish, I am better able to work through it and get through it!

2) **Acknowledge your physical pain to help confront it and ultimately, to get through it.**

   - Again, assess where the pain is coming from and what the sources may be so you can take steps to get through it.

   - Make sure you have done all you can to minimize your pain, whether it be taking medications or natural remedies in the right doses and at the right times, or getting physical therapy in the form of stretching, deep tissue massage, hot baths or whirlpool, soft ice packs, moist heat, etc.

- Share your feelings with someone you trust who is willing to really listen and who can offer feedback that is positive and encouraging.

- Whether someone is near or not, you can always speak or pray out loud to God. Our Divine Loving Creator is always present—we just may not have our "spiritual antennae" up to sense that Loving Presence.

- The most important thing is to consciously come to terms with your pain—whether you need to simply cry, moan, pray, yell, write, or tell your story. The following is an excerpt from what I've written about my own experience with pain:

The Problem of Suffering

The hottest section of the flames, the place between breaths, the pain gap—the place you get to when the physical or mental pain is so intense you're not sure if you're going to live through it. This is where I've been for several days and there are no words or gestures or even sounds that can be produced to make this more bearable. Of course I pray (and without prayer my mind would surely unravel beyond repair), but even prayer seems like a mere Band-Aid being applied to a blood-gushing wound.

To speak of my experience with chronic illness which has now become critical, without sharing the crux of my burden, this place of pain that seems humanly impossible to bear, would be like telling a story while trying to leave the main character out. Because it is this pain, this suffering, that occupies so much of the experience of illness. In his book, "The Problem of Pain," C.S. Lewis wrestles with the experience of human pain in the face of his personal faith in a Loving and Merciful Creator. Although I've not been able to read the book in its entirety, the title has been imprinted on my mind. As I walk through this fire through the searing flames of pain, I realize that pain in, and of, itself is not so horrific as pain in a state of continuum, and it is this thought that leads me to alter Lewis' title in my mind's eye to The Problem of Suffering. In my moments of less severe pain, I'm certainly braver or more stoic—so much so in fact, that most of those closest to me do not know the depth of pain and misery I experience. A close friend, who initially came into my life as a minister, has met me weekly for the past few years to help me cope with the stress and frustration of this health condition. She was visibly shocked recently when I confessed to her that I felt I could not withstand another year of this experience. She said, "You're so upbeat and caring toward everyone ... and cheerful in spite of all you're going through ... I had no idea it was this bad for you." The thing is, I find it difficult to really share with others my agony. Some of this is due to the fact that before illness became such a force in my life, I was often in the role of care-taker, nurturer, and mentor; as a mom, wife, employer, trainer and coach. So it feels upside down to be the one in need of care. But I am learning gradually to ask for help and to accept that help willingly, with gratitude. Having someone close by during these moments of teeth-gritting pain does help. Speaking out against this pain and condition helps too. And finally, keeping my spiritual eyes open even when my physical eyes are wincing shut, allows me to remember that I've survived this before and this too shall pass.

3) Acknowledge, Process, and Release Anger and Other Toxic Feelings

When we can identify the real sources of anger that we feel from the devastating effects of chronic illness, it is then easier to work through that anger—which is of vital importance. Hanging on to anger or not processing it in a healthy way can be detrimental to our health. It can cause depression, and suppress our immune systems and the production of endorphins and serotonin, as well as that of other natural healing hormones and chemicals.

It's also okay to tell God you are angry, tired, and, yes, even that you want to quit! God is Our Divine Creator, our Universal Parent, so God knows our feelings high and low, before we even recognize them. God gets it and can take the truth. I've had some Christian friends and acquaintances question whether it was okay to be angry with God or show your anger over your situation to God. One person whom I love dearly was somewhat dismayed when I told her I sometimes felt anger at God and actually spoke to God about it. She asked me, (alluding to the book of Job), "Where were you when God created the Universe?" In complete sincerity and without doubt, I replied, "With God, of course!" This thought does not reflect disrespect or irreverence to Our Beloved Creator, but, in fact, is a direct reflection of my love and faith that I like all beings, am God's Creation, and that our souls are timeless; therefore, before we became humans, we were of (with) God. Even Jesus felt anger (Mark 3:5) and, in the midst of his suffering, also questioned God (Mark 15:34).

While it is normal to sometimes feel angry at God for the suffering we experience from chronic illness, it's also vitally important for us to come to recognize that God is not the author or instigator of pain and disease—these are of earthly origin. Granted, healing does come from God, whether directly, i.e., spontaneously, without any apparent treatment or medical interventions, or indirectly, through medicine, surgery, or other specific steps or methods for healing. At some point, if we can recognize this Universal Truth, we can move on to identifying the true cause of our anger. It may be the disease or illness, or the frustration we feel from the limitations, pain, and overall losses as a result of the illness. Or perhaps it is those who may be impeding our healing in some way, such as insurance companies or health care providers who are not covering the treatments we need, or physicians who aren't really considering our needs in order to effectively treat our conditions.

Many people facing chronic illness (especially female patients) encounter medical professionals who, in their own lack of understanding about the patient's condition, may resort to blaming the patient, or accusing them of not being ill physically and even questioning their mental health. I find this especially infuriating, because my husband, who is a psychologist, and his professional colleagues, would never consider consulting with, and counseling a patient, and then after one visit, diagnosing them with MS or scleroderma. They'd never be so presumptuous as to render a diagnosis for a condition they do not specialize in! It's equally outrageous for a medical doctor with little or no training in psychology to make a snap judgment that the patient has a mental illness simply because he or she isn't familiar with the patient's disease or doesn't know how to treat the patient.

Forgiveness is a crucial part of processing and releasing anger, and therefore an essential element in healing and recovery. Sometimes this requires that we forgive even when the person or situation is still causing us pain. Feelings of long-term anger and resentment can actually cause disease, so you can imagine their damaging effect on a body that is already battling to overcome disease. Many things can be done to help work through pain and to allow ourselves to forgive, from working with a balanced, healthy, spiritually-based counselor, to doing anger exercises to reading books, or the many scriptures that teach about this topic.

The one thing that has helped me the most in the practice of forgiveness is to really focus on compassion and understanding. For example, thinking of those who have hurt me, from a purely loving standpoint (as a devoted parent would do for her child) in order to view these individuals with compassion. To remind me that they are human and realize that I truly want them to be healed, enlightened, and blessed. In situations where the hurt or disappointment runs deep, I have found that while I, in and of myself, may fall short in the ability to completely forgive, when I call upon the Holy Spirit (the Loving Essence of God) to work through me and empower me, I am able to move beyond my sole attempts.

When I acknowledge what Jesus went through so all humans could be forgiven, and recall the infinite number of times that Our Loving Creator has truly forgiven me, I better understand my need to forgive others. When I am able to reach out from a place of pure love without thoughts of piety or martyrdom, and love someone who has hurt or disappointed me I am able to experience more joy and peace. There is a scene in the movie *Castaway* where Chuck Noland (Tom Hanks' character) faces his girlfriend, Kelly Frears, (played by Helen Hunt) for the first time after surviving a plane crash that left him stranded on an island for four years. Kelly had eventually moved on with her life, as others told her that Chuck had surely died when the plane crashed into the ocean. The film lets us know that both individuals are feeling hurt, confused, and perhaps a little betrayed by fate and by time as Kelly has married and had a baby by the time she and Chuck are reunited. When the two finally come face-to-face you don't know if they're going to admonish each other, or cry out loud as they struggle for the right words. Then, Kelly grabs Chuck and just hugs him, forcing him to hug her in return. Feelings and words seem to meld quietly into that loving embrace. It impressed upon me the power of love in the face of suffering. In a way, it reminds me of the game of rock, paper, and scissors. Love, simple and sometimes even fragile, is like the paper that gently but powerfully covers the rock, diffusing the rough and hard edges of our pain.

Compassion is integral in forgiving others, and also myself, from the frustration I feel over the health challenges I'm facing. To feel compassion and empathy instead of self-loathing for what I'm going through, is essential in helping me to separate who I am from the illness that I'm experiencing. Finally, I must say that forgiving is one of the most powerful things we can do as humans. It releases us from the burden of being caught up in anger, blame, shame, and other energy-draining feelings. It gives us freedom of spirit. One thing is for certain: it will be very difficult to heal physically if you are not healing mentally, emotionally, and spiritually. When we are able to process anger in a healthy way and truly forgive, this paves the way for our physical healing.

Grieving for the things we've lost through chronic health challenges is normal and a natural part of the healing process. In fact, if we don't sort through these losses and face our feelings, they can become an emotional infection just festering beneath the surface. When we fail to recognize and process our grief, it is much like suppressing our feelings of anger, in that it can lower our immune systems and suppress endorphins and other healing chemicals that our bodies are naturally programmed to release. At some point, we hope to find a place where the mourning becomes less a part of our journey and gives way to thoughts of a new life and a chance to co-create new beginnings—even if they are entirely different from anything we have previously experienced.

4) **Seek Sound Guidance and Support.**

In addition to your spouse or caregiver, enlist another person who is emotionally unattached to your situation and who can give sound advice, feedback, and support. This can be a professional counselor or psychologist, a minister or lay minister, or a support group leader. This individual should be available either in person or by telephone if you experience a crisis. Keep their contact information nearby at all times.

5) **Humor.**

The sunny side of life is often found through the funny side of life. Being able to look at a difficult situation from a humorous viewpoint can be literally lifesaving. Laughing and being silly helps us to lighten our outlook and puts things in a better perspective. My husband and I regularly play nostalgic, upbeat music and often break into a ludicrous-looking tap dance routine, especially considering neither of us has had tap lessons nor has the slightest idea of what is required to render authentic tap steps!. As writers who love humor, we also do some pretty wacky impressions and character skits. This not only boosts our morale but also stimulates those all-important endorphins. Perhaps most significantly, this behavior also defies the energy behind illness and strife, which actually serves to promote healing and recovery. I remember watching a story about some Mount McKinley climbers who were stranded overnight just below the summit. They made a conscious effort to joke with one another while facing the possibility of death from hypothermia and dehydration, and later said it was this attitude that truly fortified their spirits and was an essential factor in their survival.

Avoiding the Emergency Exit

There may be times when we have done everything we know to do to survive the pitfalls of chronic illness and are still overwhelmed by it all. Almost everyone hits that rock-bottom place of despair at some time during long-term illness. In these moments, the pain and suffering may seem so intense that virtually anything that can remove us from this place seems like relief, from taking unprescribed drugs to numb our pain to intentionally wanting to take an overdose of drugs to end it all. When any means of release seems inviting or inevitable, it's time to signal 911 and let someone who can help be aware of our crisis. I should be an expert on this topic by now. After seven years of chronic illness that has too often turned critical, and with limited treatment options for my condition through conventional medicine and health insurance, I have many times found myself in that rock-bottom place. It is, quite honestly, a living hell, when you wake up and realize, "Oh God. This is NOT a nightmare—it is my life!"

It is in these moments, when all hope seems lost forever that we are most vulnerable. Sometimes this can occur simply from experiencing a long bout with intense pain, or from having gone without enough sleep. Pain and fatigue can rob us of hope, peace, and clarity. Also, not eating properly and being short of vital nutrients can trigger depression, more pain or fatigue, and that hopeless feeling. A series of events may also bring on that utter sense of hopelessness. As I write this, we are living with my husband's parents (who have become so dear to me that they are now simply "Mom" and "Dad"). After we lost our lovely home due to excessive medical bills and no health insurance, we rented for a while. Later, when my husband was hired at a university in our hometown of Houston, we moved back and found that his parents needed our assistance and we needed theirs. The family home is very old but has the architectural charm typical of 100-year-old houses. Initially, we thought we would have the opportunity to renovate, but after contributing to several improvements and repairs, we realized that the house would require hundreds of thousands of dollars to put it right again. As my health seemed to decline and out-of-pocket expenses for treatment and medication mounted up, we dealt with one problem at a time. But in the past year this old house really put our sanity and our pocketbooks to the test. Within just a few months we had to replace several air conditioning units, and then a gas line ruptured. We were apparently Divinely Blessed that we all did not blow up from the leaking gas. The gas lines had to be replaced by new electric lines. That in turn, required new electric water heaters, stoves, and the replacement of all appliances running on gas. For several weeks, we went with no hot water or stoves to cook on. Washing dishes, bathing, and doing laundry in nineteenth-century style required twice the time and energy.

In the midst of all this, Mom had a terrible fall outside a store and has had to receive ongoing physical therapy. Then, Dad, as if not to be outdone, had an awful fall in his bathroom that sent him to the hospital with a dislocated shoulder, broken arm, and other injuries. After a few weeks, he was transferred to a hospice for rehabilitative care for several months. I jokingly told them both that if they wanted to try out for the Senior Olympics, we should start at the beginning and gradually train for these extreme falls instead of literally diving in headfirst! My husband and I had to step up our support with extra cooking, grocery shopping and other errands, as well as overseeing the installation of electric lines and appliances to the house. Mom already had her plate full, trying to recover from her fall and going back and forth to the hospital to be with Dad. One morning, as my husband attempted to remove all the water heaters in the house to save on expenses, the nozzle on the heater in our kitchen came off in his hands. We spent close to an hour trying to catch the gushing water in large trash bins and pouring it out the back door and down the sink, and finally cleaning up the excess water. While it seems almost comical to envision it now, it was really stressful at the time because William was teaching about three times the class hours of most professors, and I was coping with the withdrawal symptoms from slowly weaning off of the prednisone, and other health challenges. These series of unfortunate events would have been a considerable strain on any family, but with the chronic illness factoring in, it all seemed unbearable.

Another hope-draining experience that has occurred on numerous occasions is when our search for viable medical treatment results in yet another doctor not having enough knowledge or understanding to help me. To make matters worse, many of us who experience chronic illness have encountered a physician who is too proud or fearful to admit that he or she doesn't understand how to treat our condition, and instead resorts to the underhanded tactic of pronouncing that the illness doesn't exist, or that our condition is psychological as opposed to physiological. Of course, unless this physician has an extensive background in psychology or psychiatry, or is a psychologist or psychiatrist, they are incapable of making such a determination. Unfortunately, there are far too many reports of this type of improper medical practice, which can be devastating to the chronically ill patient, and to her or his loved ones. It can leave one questioning their own sanity if they are not strongly grounded in who they are and confident in understanding what they are going through. If you and your loved one(s) know you have a condition and find upon visiting a new doctor that he or she attempts to dismiss your health concerns by suggesting that you have a psychological disorder, ask that doctor to provide you with his or her credentials for treating psychological or psychiatric disorders.

Sometimes, other issues may instigate feelings of despair and hopelessness. There have been instances when I have seen my precious husband feeling so sad for what I'm going through, and so overwhelmed from working extra hours to pay for expensive and uninsured treatments, that I start wondering if perhaps we'd all be better off if I were out of the picture! That "noble ego" leaves me thinking, "Your husband and everyone who cares for you would be better off if you'd just go ahead and die!" This typically occurs when the bad days outnumber the good, and the effort to just get up and out to do the simplest of errands or tasks seems to take more than I have. It's only in these moments when things seem unbearable and nothing in my life seems to make sense anymore that thoughts about whether or not I can go on filter in. It is as if I'm standing on the edge of the world, and with just one step forward, I could plummet out of this place of suffering. I can candidly say that as a faith-based person, I don't believe that putting an end to one's life is God's true plan for us. I am not someone who would be thought of as suicidal. In fact, two of my closest friends who have stood by me through the worst of the difficult moments insist that I am one of the strongest spirits they have ever known. Patty*, who has worked in healing ministry for years, says, "I've never known any-

---

*   name changed

one to have as strong and persevering spirit as yours." Marilyn*, who went through a seven-year sojourn alongside her late husband as he battled cancer, and who still lovingly nurtures so many, simply says that William and I are her "heroes and inspiration." Then there is my friend from Central America, Natia*, who saw me one day when I was feeling overcome by symptoms and in the initial phases of recovering from my multiple fractures. I was truly ready to quit, but Natia said, "Jamey, you cannot let this thing win, you are like a beautiful oak tree with great branches, offering love and shelter to so many ... we need you here in this world and you must continue to get strength from your spiritual roots!" Sometimes these responses sound bizarre to me. Are they really talking about me, when I seem to be so broken—physically and mentally? Then there are times when I believe they are right. Yes, I have a tenacious spirit—many who have witnessed what I have been through say they are amazed that I have survived such trauma. I can also say that when I am confronted with months and even years of ongoing suffering from chronic pain, and the harsh reality of the physical deterioration of my body from the effects of illness (that, as yet, has limited treatment options) it can, and has, deflated my optimism and chiseled away at my determination. It is at these times, when doubt comes pouring in like flood waters, that even the most faithful and persevering people can crumble. I have been at this crumbling place (as has my not completely indomitable spirit) more times than I would like to admit!

So, how have I made it past all those dark nights of the soul? Why am I still here today after facing so many gut-wrenching, seemingly unbearable moments? How is it that this body has held up through so many 911 moments, both in the ER and outside of the hospital, continuing the act of living months and even years after some *medical experts* have deemed me to be breaths away from no more breaths? So far, mercy and grace have filtered into these 911 moments, somehow steering me through the darkness and pain and giving me glimpses of heaven in the midst of hell.

6) Pray for (Believe and Receive) Divine Help.

I don't want this to sound like a platitude or glib in any way because, when we are at that "crumbling place" and feel as though our feet are surely going to slip off the precipice of life, (or we feel the urge to jump off the cliff) just the thought of one more prayer, one more petition, to Our Divine but invisible Creator may seem futile. However, it is exactly in these most despairing of moments, as I am able to press into prayer, that miracles (although sometimes visibly undetectable) most often occur. When I pray and confess to my Loving Holy Parent-Creator that it seems as if I can't go on, and ask the Holy Spirit (God's Loving Essence) to help me, I find that I am indeed somehow lifted up and out of that place of dark despair. Sometimes I sense that Loving Presence fill me with strength right away and actually ease my symptoms. Then, there are other times when I feel as though there is no response ... but, eventually, maybe minutes, hours, or even days, later, I do feel the peace and comfort of Divine Love and strength again. The truth is, no matter what affliction, trouble, or iniquity, you may be battling, God's Loving Presence is there for each of us—no matter what. All we have to do is ask and we eventually realize that Divine Love never leaves us, but sometimes our pain and despair can block out our reception. It is as though our spiritual antennas aren't receiving or are being blocked by static in the form of pain, fatigue, and so on. However, if we keep searching for that clear station that channels the voice of God's Love, the static will abate, and this is when we really feel the amazing effects of healing and hope flowing through us.

7) Call in Reliable Reinforcements.

Sometimes I have the insight, courage, and discipline to reach out for help by calling a loved one, or, if the hour is late, a help hotline, or a prayer helpline. Speaking with someone who cares often changes my outlook. Avoid calling someone who is ill-equipped to help you. Once I was going through a terrible episode with symptoms and exhausted from pain and fatigue. I didn't want my husband to see me in such a state, so I got in our car and started driving. I was crying so hard that I was having a difficult time seeing clearly, so I pulled over and phoned a close relative. When I told her I didn't think I could go another hour like this, she admonished me with a curt reply, "Oh, snap out of it! You just need to get a grip and start thinking about how your husband and everyone else would feel if you check out!" This is not the type of "help" or "encouragement" one needs when they are overwhelmed and feeling that they are incapable of going on. Ironically, just a year earlier, I accompanied this relative to her chemotherapy sessions and to appointments with various specialists as she went through treatments for cancer (thankfully, from which she had recovered). There were many days and nights throughout that time when I offered her a shoulder to lean on and encouraged her when the effects of chemotherapy left her feeling weak and down. Never would I have dreamed of telling her during those difficult moments to "just snap out of it!" But that is my point, some people can receive caregiving but are not equipped to reciprocate. It is important for us to know who we can turn to in our most difficult moments and whom to avoid.

8) **Use Your Voice of Reason.**

There are other times when I've reasoned with myself, "Okay. You've got to tend to those cards, gifts, and letters that are stacked up waiting to be sent to your loved ones, or get the bills and paperwork in order so your husband and family can find everything, and THEN, if you still feel you can't be here and do this anymore, then, well...." And of course, a day or two later, something has occurred to give me a little more strength, a little more hope.

9) **Physically Move Out of That Sick Space.**

When we are feeling overcome by despair and inclined to take drastic measures to find relief, it can be lifesaving to move our bodily selves to another space. If you can't get out of your home, move to another place in it or, walk outside. Open a window or door and let the outside air in. If you can actually get out, then going to a place nearby such as a park or library, where there are other people, can move our minds out of the despair mode. The sky, birds, plants, and flowers can fill us with signs of joyful life.

10) **Offer Solace and Compassion When You Need It Most.**

While it may sound impossible or even ludicrous, the act of reaching out—yes, while facing our own dire circumstances—and helping someone else who is in need can prove to empower us with love and an inner strength and purpose that can conquer those feelings of despair. Studies have concluded that when we help someone by rendering an unexpected kindness we actually experience the physical benefit of increasing endorphin levels not only in ourselves but also in the person(s) we are helping. And, amazingly, if others simply witness this exchange, they too, can experience an endorphin rush! There have been times when I have been in the midst of terrible pain and a flare-up of symptoms to the point where I had trouble thinking straight, but have reached really deep inside to find the strength to minister to someone near me. For instance, sometimes when my mother-in-love is really going through a difficult time with her own pain or fatigue, I have drawn on my knowledge as a fitness trainer and my experience in physical rehabilitation to give her deep tissue massage and help her stretch her aching muscles. Sometimes I just sit with her and put light pressure on the areas where she is hurting while praying aloud with her for the pain to leave. And gentle hugs and shared prayers go a long way to lift up her spirits as well as those of other loved ones.

Other times, I may just lean on that Divine Love and power to give me the strength to cook or bake something for my family. It's especially revitalizing for me to offer care in some way to those who care for me. Even if I find myself confined to bed, I can still listen to my husband as he discusses how his day has gone or a work matter that concerns him. I encourage him to eat right, exercise, and visit with his friends. Whenever I'm not in a critical phase with illness, I run little errands: I go to the grocery store, purchase some clothing he may need, or buy him some little token such as his favorite scented soap. Sometimes I'm able to contribute to his writing or speaking projects with feedback, or with ideas or editing.

It is also empowering and uplifting to help those who may not be in our inner circle of family and loved ones. I have committed to be on phone standby for several friends who either head up support groups for individuals with various chronic diseases, or are lay ministers. As a professional speaker and someone who has done many interviews for my writing projects, I am a good listener and when needed, can offer some insight and feedback. But let me say that you need not be a great speaker, or even very articulate, to offer a listening ear and a comforting shoulder to someone. This can be done on the phone or even online if you and the other person are not able to be in each other's physical presence. My contacts also know to inform me if the person who needs to be reached needs an immediate response, or can be called within a day or two. Then, depending on my circumstances, I can let them know if I can connect with the person they are referring to me in sufficient time. I do know that whenever I'm able to just push through my situation and lend a compassionate ear, I always end up feeling better physically, mentally, and spiritually.

I'll never forget our harrowing evacuation attempt when Hurricane Rita threatened to hit Houston with a level five impact. Everyone was asked to exit the city in a specific order, with those closest to the coast leaving first and so on. My husband and I felt we had no choice but to evacuate, because of the serious health challenges both his parents were facing, and my health problems. With approximately 1 to 2 million or more trying to get out of the city, we knew it would be a long and difficult drive from Houston to Fort Worth, where my sister and my husband's aunt had opened their homes to us. It turned out to be a living nightmare for us and for many, many other families as eight-lane freeways and toll roads turned into parking lots. Cars overheated, gas ran out, and we passengers experienced heat exhaustion and dehydration as there were no public restrooms available for many miles and hours. With the help of my brother-in-love text messaging via our cell phone, we were able to find a back route out of the city after about ten hours on the road. Unfortunately, that route was also extremely congested with thousands of fellow evacuees.

Once again, we found our drive alternating between a complete stand still and moving at snail's pace. After a few hours of that, I began to dehydrate and the extreme heat took a toll on my health; my body felt as if an electrical shock was going through me, and feeling extreme heat one minute and a clammy cold the next. My head felt as if tiny explosions were going off inside my brain. Mom, a retired nurse, was sitting beside me in the cramped back seat, told my husband that I was exhibiting the signs of someone having a mild stroke. I could see William's eyes looking at me in the rearview mirror and knew he was terribly worried and trying to decide what to do next. Mom and I held hands and began praying—she, out loud and I, silently. I could see my husband agonizing over what to do; just turning the air conditioning on would have been taking a risk that the car would overheat again and possibly stop running. Meanwhile, on the single-lane road, people who were panicking or just unwilling to wait along with the rest of us were passing rows of cars in the oncoming lane, putting everyone in danger and cutting in front of families that had been waiting much longer.

Within just minutes of experiencing that terrible episode, we came upon a family on the side of the road who were literally begging for someone to stop and jump-start their car. Typically, we would have offered help without a second thought, but again, I could see William's face looking back at me and knew he was thinking, "If we help these people, we will lose our place in line on the road and have a longer delay if we need emergency medical assistance for Jamey." As our eyes locked, I felt a complete sense of peace. I knew somehow I'd be all right, and whispered to William to stop and help that family. He understood and pulled over. As he helped the stranded drivers attach cables to their battery, I could feel the strange symptoms subsiding. By the time the other family's car was running again, my body seemed to pull out of the crisis mode. Another driver who had observed the situation let us right back into the long line of cars on the road. Only about a dozen cars had moved ahead! Amazingly, just a few yards down the road, another vehicle was stalled and no one was stopping to help the occupants. Once again, we pulled off the road to help get this car started, and once again, another driver let us right back into the line. We had been on the road for over 14 hours and it took another 8½ hours to reach our destination. (In normal circumstances, the entire trip would have taken only four or five hours.) Although we were all exhausted and dehydrated, and experiencing considerable muscle pain, other than a very bloodshot eye and a sort of foggy state of mind, I had no more stroke-like signs. We knew that miracles had happened during that trip and that offering help to others when it seemed least doable had strengthened and blessed us.

You may actually be strengthened, and comforted, by offering someone else solace when you need it yourself. Or, as Pastor Joel Osteen of Lakewood Church (www.lakewood.cc) said in one of his recently televised sermons, "Sow a seed when you are most in need." That said, also bear in mind that you should not feel pressured or obligated to do this every time that you find yourself in the midst of a critical flare-up. I am not always able to do this—sometimes the pain or physical weakness is just too much but I hold on to the fact that there are many times when I have been able to reach out to someone else in the face of my own needs, and that has always resulted in some kind of a healing blessing.

Hope: Antidote to Hopelessness and Key to Recovery

It is the worst place to be but one that almost everyone who has ever dealt with chronic illness has been—that place where we feel void of hope. So where do we find hope in a place that seems empty of this life-changing energy? Hope can come from many places, and often from a source that we least expect.

No matter what, keep the flame of hope alive. The following list has proven helpful for me and my family as well as for some of the people we've met who are coping with chronic illness:

> **Assist List**—Enlist others, such as friends, family, church members, or volunteers at medical support groups or area hospitals, to help in your journey as you continue to seek professional medical help. Breakthroughs in treatments for both traditional and nontraditional diseases are being made all the time. For instance, one of the conditions I have been diagnosed with recently had no known name or support organization seven years ago. But because we were open about my condition and symptoms (and the struggles that we were going through in searching for answers and possible treatments) with friends and family who were close to us, we had a network of "eyes and ears" working on our behalf. Subsequently, our reverend, and his wife, saw a news report that featured some individuals who had the exact same symptoms and health problems that I was suffering from, and they phoned us that night to tell us about the program. We soon learned that a support organization had been founded several years earlier that had more than 10,000 individuals registered, who apparently shared the same condition. In the last year, three different medical experts in three different states have begun researching this disease for possible treatments and cures. The more people you know who are trustworthy, who are aware of your condition, the more possibilities there are that someone may come across something that will help in your treatment. It also is comforting to know that there are people who care about your

quest for recovery and are consciously and graciously onboard with that process.

> **Gratitude for Gifts**—Sometimes, just focusing on a few things from my mental list of blessings, or gifts that I have to be thankful for, helps to change my outlook. This takes focus and fortitude when we are struggling in those darkest moments, but there's always SOMETHING to be thankful for and when we recognize this it can lift our spirits.

> **Favor**—A few years ago, I was fortunate to hear a wonderful message by Bishop T.D. Jakes of The Potter's House Ministry (www.thepottershouse. org), who defined *favor* as looking back on better times and drawing on those memories as a tool to get us through the drought. This helps us to keep our vision and believe that things will once again be better at some time in the future. When I step out of my current physical and mental state, I can look back on the wonderful times I've had with my husband, family, and friends. Sharing their company has provided me with precious memories. Raising my daughter and watching her grow into a lovely young woman has also given me that all important reflection of "favor." Thinking about the many opportunities I've had to help others through writing and speaking, and coaching clients in improving their health and physical condition, also lifts my spirit. When I recall my past work with students through interactive workshops that encouraged them to embrace their unique identity and gifts, I am infused with hope again. I can also draw strength from believing that the future will bring relief, improvement, and even miracles for healing and renewal. Christian author, Philip Yancey, refers to this as "future faith" in his book, *Reaching for the Invisible God* (Zondervan 2001).

> **Outside Sources of Inspiration**—Seek to meet and get to know others who have made it through a similar health challenge. This may be a friend or acquaintance or someone you've met through a support group. Read stories and scriptures, and watch documentaries or true-to-life movies of other people experiencing miraculous breakthroughs and healing. As I make the final editing changes on this section of the book, CNN is airing a tribute to honor a handful of everyday *Heroes*. Many of these individuals have overcome unimaginable challenges to help others or to improve conditions in the world. Their stories remind me that Grace and healing can flow through virtually anyone and any circumstance.

> **Creativity**—Creating or using our Divine Gifts and talents can give us renewed purpose, and hope, and invigorate our souls and bodies. You may love gardening and watching things grow. If your condition prevents you from getting outside frequently, bring some hanging plants or small potted flowers or herbs indoors. Living plants are also natural air filters so your physical senses can benefit, as well as your mind and soul. If music is your forte, have a portable keyboard or smaller instrument to play to ignite your inner light. Drawing or painting is another way to express yourself creatively without a lot of physical exertion. On stronger health days I love to get in the kitchen and cook or bake something. As part of my work, I taught workshops on cooking and baking "clean" (healthier versions of our favorite foods). So, when I cook, or bake with organic and natural ingredients I am buoyed by the fact that my family will enjoy what I've made and be nourished as well. Take special precautions to maximize your energy when choosing creative outlets. For instance, when I'm in the kitchen, I use a high stool with castor rollers, so I can work at the counter without causing undue stress on my back or legs. As mentioned before, writing or journaling is a good way to express yourself, and helps to work through issues at the same time. If you are good with tools, you may find solace in repairing small things around the house. There are so many possibilities for tapping into your creative nature—let it be an invigorating part of your healing experience.

> **Rid, Recycle, and Renew**—In between the more critical moments of flare-ups with symptoms and pain, try to get rid of one thing each week if possible, that you are no longer using. Those items that have gathered dust, stopped working, or, are just no longer useful in your present life should be removed. Giving away or recycling items signifies the vital message to yourself, your family and loved ones, and to Our Divine Creator, that you are not living in the past or being impeded by clutter. Likewise, at least once per month, replace something that is worn out or no longer works efficiently in your life. This can be anything from a lamp to a worn-out pair of shoes. By signifying that you are consistently renewing things in your life and keeping things around you in good working order, you also remain mindful of your own physical, mental, and spiritual renewal.

> **Seeking Peace and Realizing (God) Love**—Knowing that the Divine forces of Love are actually within our bodies and minds at all times can be life-saving in the midst of the critical or most difficult times of ill-

ness. When Jesus said, "I will never leave you or forsake you," (Hebrews 13:5), He meant that He would be available through the Spirit to all He knew then (especially the poor, afflicted, socially outcast and so on), and to all who would come after Him, in the centuries to follow. It has taken some years for me to begin to understand this Truth: no matter what I'm going through, no matter how intolerable or unbearable the pain and suffering may seem, even in that very moment, I am loved, and I have love in my heart for my precious Sacred Father-Mother Creator and for many people—those in my life at the present and for those who were blessings in my past, for their loving energy continues to reside in my heart forever. Whenever I can quiet my soul just long enough to grab hold of this amazing Truth, that Love is within me and all around me even in the midst of what seems like utter chaos, then Peace prevails over my situation and that opens the door to the miracles of overcoming illness and ultimately, healing.

The Waiting Place:

For those of us going through the challenges and trials of chronic illness, we often experience the frustration of "not doing." We may have to withstand many hours, weeks, months, or even years of the exhausting elements of pain, fatigue and physical limitations that are part of managing and coping with symptoms that prevent us from doing the things we feel called to do. This is where a type 'A' personality such as mine can be supremely tested, although I'm gradually learning to seek peace and even joy while in a holding pattern with my health, and to find ways to enjoy aspects of my life even through long bouts of suffering. In what seems like a long pause in my life, I still battle with the urge to fix things or insist upon answers and relief. I jokingly tell friends that I am a "recovering type A." There's nothing wrong with wanting, praying, claiming, and even expecting to heal and fully recover, and I believe without a doubt that this IS God's best plan for each of us. But we also need to come to terms with the fact that our healing may not be spontaneous or instantaneous, and therefore we have to find some degree of peace and acceptance that our healing could take much more time and effort than we had ever anticipated. And it may come in ways that we did not exactly expect or envision.

I still struggle some days to fight off feelings of frustration when I am unable to be productive due to illness. Part of this desire is really very natural; I, like many people feel fulfilled when I'm doing something positive or accomplishing tasks and goals. It is our nature to want to evolve and therefore, to want to achieve, not just for ourselves but for those around us. Our minds and physical senses drive us to want to do something that tells us that we are viable beings in this world. But it is our souls that enable us to be still and just "be" regardless of whether or not we are "doing." I've heard others refer to this by surmising that we are not "Human Doings" but "Human Beings." When we are in the midst of a difficult flare-up of symptoms and we are willing to set aside our impatient desires "to do" or accomplish specific tasks, we may find a deeper sense of serenity and understanding while being in the waiting place.

Believe in your healing and recovery, not in the disease.

When we battle chronic illness on a long-term basis, it is easy to lose our personal vision of health—how we looked, felt, and interacted in this world when we were healthier. We can be like the lab rat that over time is so conditioned by being locked inside a cage when the door is opened, he doesn't even have the mindset to leave his cage. As humans it is our nature or natural instinct to form our reality based on what we see day after day. But our vision for healing is crucial and we have to consciously envision our bodies and minds being healed. One of the most difficult aspects of my experience with chronic illness as it has become critical from the effects of toxic medication has been maintaining the image of a "healthy me." Mental discipline and exercises are far more difficult to master than physical exercise, but the greatest power for healing our bodies comes from within our minds. To help me to focus on an inner image of my body being healed and becoming strong and fit again, my husband copied some photos of me that were taken to promote several wellness and *Clean Food©* workshops that I presented just before ill-prescribed medicine drastically altered my health and appearance. He typed, "This is THE REAL YOU" on top of the photos and placed them in different areas around our home. I also have several pictures of myself in better health alongside some photos of my family sharing "well times" on our refrigerator and on the wall adjacent to my bedside. Every day I see these and affirm that I will recover. While I can reclaim physical health and my "healthy image," I understand that I will not be the exact same person in those pictures because of what I've been through from the illness. I have gained insight, patience, and a stronger sense of being—which will be an integral part of the healthier me. In addition to using personal photos to help you in visualizing, you can cut out images from magazines that inspire thoughts of healing that are specific to your circumstances.

Envision.

With your mind's eye (or spiritual eyes), envision every cell, every organ, all your bodily tissues and your health systems, such as your immune, endocrine, respiratory, and nervous systems, being bathed in the Holy Spirit of Divine Love (or your Higher Power). I see the Loving Life Force of Jesus, which His unconditional love and sacrifice have made available to me, shining in the center of all my cells, perfecting all that concerns me.

Imagine.

Use your imagination to visualize your body in optimum health, then put that image into actual scenes that you want to live out. For this to work for me, I have to discipline myself to get quiet several times each day. This is usually when I first wake up and when I'm going to bed, but also sometimes in the middle of my day, if I find myself too focused on health challenges or other stressful situations. As I breathe deeply and open my heart, mind, and being to Divine Love, I begin to see mental images of myself healed, in specific scenarios from my life over a period of time; from as early as the coming year, to various junctures in the future with my husband and other loved ones. I imagine walking with my husband at that athletic pace that I was previously capable of. I see us in my mind's eye shooting baskets at the park or walking hand-in-hand in another city on a leisurely trip overseas, such as Italy and Greece. I envision myself conducting a wellness workshop and speaking in front of a large group again, inspiring and being inspired.

William and I regularly think of one to three images in the near future with me fully recovered and us living lives free of chronic illness, and we share these images out loud to each other at night before going to bed. We describe such scenes as bouncing on the bed in our beautiful new home with, yes, *our future children* (to whom we've already assigned names) and reading them a story. Coming home from a trip where we've jointly given a workshop or presentation. Picking scented flowers and placing them all around our home, cooking a healthy dinner with organic herbs from our garden with all our kids, family and friends present. The more you practice this process, the more natural it will become to you. There truly is power in our thoughts and our spiritual vision; this is a Universal Truth that has been apparent to many through the ages.

Keep a Healthy Distance from Naysayer's and Doubters.

Along this odyssey, we have encountered various people (acquaintances, and even some family members and friends), who simply don't get our strong belief that God *can* and *will* deliver us from this place and, in time, heal me as an individual, and us, as a family. And as with Job, Our Loving Creator will bring us to an even better life than we had before the storm of chronic illness left our lives as we had known them strewn about in pieces. While we try to find joy and peace, and meaning in each day in the midst of chronic illness, we also pray for and focus on believing in, receiving, and giving thanks in advance for, miraculous recovery and renewal. The naysayer's will inevitably advise us to not get our hopes too high, or will say that miracles are something of the past, but we know that all things are possible to those who love God. And I love what television minister, Joyce Meyer (joycemeyerministries.org), once said: "I'd rather ask God for everything and get some of it, than ask God for nothing and get all of it!"

Backup Caregiver and Counsel:

In addition to your established or main caregiver, whether it be your spouse or another family member or friend, it is vitally important to find a back-up caregiver who can offer you information, compassion, feed-back, and support. The backup caregiver can provide you with assistance and care when your main caregiver is busy or just needs a break. It also allows you to experience other relationships, and interaction with more than one person. Set up an arrangement with your backup caregiver to meet once a week and to visit by phone several times each week. If you are well enough to get out, treat her or him to a hot tea, coffee, or smoothie. Or visit a bookstore that has tables or comfortable chairs so you can sit down together and look at some books that you both find interesting. Go to a nearby arboretum, flower garden, or park. You may enjoy going to an outdoor concert or play, or to hear an inspirational lecture, or to a casual church service. Keep it simple—do things that are uplifting and that won't zap your strength. Always, always, *always* do little things to let your caregivers know how much you appreciate them and how precious their support is to you!

As mentioned earlier in this section of the book, it is important to also have someone whom you, and your primary caregiver (your spouse or other loved one) can turn to for a mutual exchange of support and counsel. If you and your spouse can find an opportunity to visit a counselor, do so. Even one visit per month can help tremendously. Look for someone who is spiritually grounded and also familiar with counseling patients who have had chronic illnesses. Your church or area churches may provide counseling services for a donation or a sliding fee of whatever you can pay. Likewise, there are some nonprofit organizations that offer counseling on a sliding scale, based on your income and what you can afford. Over the years, we have even found several counselors, who have provided sessions with us by phone when my condition prevented me from getting out of bed. This is also a great way for the well spouse to get things off of his or her chest and get some care back to them.

Support groups for the chronically ill and their spouses and families can be very helpful. Just be sure that the group is also addressing issues of recovery and treatments and providing positive feedback and inspiration, as opposed to solely dwelling on the disease and difficulties. The Internet is also a great way to find others with similar conditions, the latest research and treatment options, support groups in your area, and even chat rooms for patients and care providers.

Your *outlook* is a key factor in how well you navigate through the illness and, in your chances for recovery.

While it is easy to feel overwhelmed and even defeated from the long-term effects of chronic illness—especially when we are going through a critical phase, it is so important to our survival and recovery process to try and maintain an optimistic outlook. "You can get bitter or better." I'm not sure who originally coined this phrase, but I first heard it spoken by Natalie Cole while watching a biography of her life. For those who haven't heard Natalie's story, it is truly a testament to the power of love, forgiveness, and perseverance. Natalie recovered from depression, drug addiction, and the pain of being neglected as a child. She is a living example of how we can choose to get better instead of letting bitterness and unforgivingness rob us of peace, healing, and happiness.

No matter how critical our health may be or how much we may suffer, we can choose the way in which we respond to this experience. It is that choice that will dictate how we get through the trial. Within a short period of time, I was able to witness both ends of this spectrum. Recently I was in the checkout line at one of my favorite health food supermarkets. As we were placing my grocery bags into the cart, a man in a wheelchair came into the store through the "out" door. It was a few minutes past closing time but one of the staff who was near the door told the man he could go ahead and get a few items even though the store was closed. The woman was very friendly and certainly accommodating because, at most retail places, when a customer arrives after closing time, they are simply asked to come back the next day during store hours. The man in the wheelchair glared at the woman and cussed her out while whipping his chair around, and heading into the store. This man obviously was determined to do what he pleased without regard for anyone or anything but himself. Everyone around him (myself included) just looked on in disbelief. I told the woman that I had been confined to using a wheelchair or automated cart for over a year while healing from multiple fractures in my hip and back due to ill effects of medication. I reassured her that not everyone in that situation felt it was justification for behaving rudely, and disrespectfully, to others. The man was clearly bitter about his situation and, by his loveless attitude and behavior was making his life, and anyone who happened to be around him, needlessly miserable.

On the other side of this coin is a woman from my church, whom I had not previously met, who cheerfully came to pick me up and drive me to a medical treatment that was about an hour from her home. As Lisa (name changed), drove me back home after the treatment, we chatted about a number of things. When we arrived and she offered to help me to my door, I saw a set of crutches in the backseat. They belonged to Lisa. She, too, was battling a chronic illness that at times affected her ability to walk. Lisa would never even have mentioned her own illness as she assisted me had I not asked her directly about the crutches. I later heard that Lisa had traveled to Louisiana to help those who had suffered losses from Hurricane Katrina. In spite of her own health challenges, Lisa had clearly chosen the better over the bitter.

Find that place between acknowledging your pain and illness, and putting too much focus on your condition and circumstances.

While we want to think and speak positive thoughts for healing and recovery, it's important not to be in denial about what we are experiencing. I have a dear friend who believes (as I do) that our words and thoughts can affect our actual experience. But there have been times when I have needed to update her about the status of my health and she has interrupted with a cheerleader's voice to insist that "We're not claiming *that* or giving it energy!" There is a place between acknowledging the actual, current state of our condition, and dwelling on the problems or giving more attention or energy to the disease than to our recovery. Sometimes we need to discuss where we are at (that moment) with our family, physicians, or friends who are in a position to help whether by actually providing care, treatment, or simply praying for healing for our specific situation. Also, part of being compassionate and supportive is being able to listen. Once information has been communicated, both parties can agree to pray for, and believe in, your healing, and, that it is already taking place. Those in ministry of any kind need to be cautious not to turn the concept of positive affirming thoughts for healing, or the possibility of spontaneous healing, into an energy of condemnation. I've heard from a number of people who are seeking renewed health and deliverance from chronic illness, who truly believe that spontaneous healing can come directly from God. But when they did not heal or improve, immediately after someone laid hands on them or anointed them with oil and healing prayer, they felt that there was something wrong with their faith. As I've come to understand, some people heal from a specific condition after a dose of medicine or just a few treatments, while others may require many doses of medication as well as a long series of health treatments. This principle holds true in direct, or Divine Healing, where some may be able to receive healing virtually instantaneously while others may need ongoing prayers and anointing over a period of time in order to fully recover their health and well-being. Also, everyone involved needs to acknowledge that the Divine Gift of Healing can be experienced through doctors, treatments, and medicine (conventional or holistic), as well as directly from God, without any apparent worldly conduits. *The Healing Light* (First Ballantine/Epiphany 1983, 1980) by Agnes Sanford, offers some practical advice on the topic of Divine Healing. The most important thing to remember is that every person is different so one's experience in recovery will also vary as to how, and when, she or he will receive renewed health. The important thing is that we continue to strive toward that healing place by doing all that we can to heal in the physical realm while also keeping our spiritual eyes focused on our road to recovery.

About the Authors

Dr. William July

William July, Ph.D. has a special interest in the psychology of relationships. He is the author of several books on relationships published by Doubleday, including a national bestseller. For titles, see the front of this book. William regularly appears on CNN, the Fox News Channel, and other news networks providing insights on current issues. Also, he is a featured relationship and personal coach for the Great Day Houston Show on KHOU (CBS). He writes a column for *Our Texas* magazine and has also been a columnist for *Essence* magazine.

Dr. July is a member of the American Psychological Association, the Society for Personality & Social Psychology, and the International Association for Relationship Research. In addition to his media work he has authored a chapter on personality psychology for a textbook published by Pearson, a leading academic publisher.

Jamey Lacy July

Jamey Lacy July is a certified fitness specialist, former competitive athlete and fitness model who has been featured in magazines such as *SHAPE* and *Muscle & Fitness*. She established Houston's first full-scale personal training and physical rehabilitation center. Jamey has authored numerous articles on topics of physical and spiritual wellness and lectured nationally for organizations such as The Institute of Medicine and The Women's Sports Foundation. She has appeared often on television and was the subject of an interview that won Best Sports Story by the Associated Press.

As a consumer advocate, Jamey has lobbied Congress to promote legislation for safer health issues for Americans. In *A Husband, A Wife, and An Illness*, Jamey reveals the irony and raw nature of her plight with a ravaging illness while also offering helpful insights for surviving the critical phases of chronic diseases.

Photo of Jamey during early stage of illness before onset of most severe symptoms.*

---

*   For an up-to-date timeline of photos, visit CouplesFacingIllness.com

For More Information and Support, Visit CouplesFacingIllness.com

CouplesFacingIllness.com provides information and support to couples living with chronic illness. At the website you'll find content such as:

- Links to articles of interest for couples facing illness
- Links to resources
- Inspirational material
- Free audio clips that you can listen to online or download
- A blog where you can post your own thoughts, feelings, or ideas on various discussion topics

CouplesFacingIllness.com

978-0-595-44726-8
0-595-44726-0

5222113R0

Made in the USA
Lexington, KY
16 April 2010